Wonders

Close Reading Companion

Mc
Graw
Hill
Education

Cover and Title pages: Nathan Love

www.mheonline.com/readingwonders

Send all inquiries to:
McGraw-Hill Education
Two Penn Plaza
New York, New York 10121

ISBN: 978-0-02-130521-6
MHID: 0-02-130521-8

Printed in the United States of America.

11 12 13 14 LMN 22 21 20 19 18

E

Getting to Know Us

Our Community

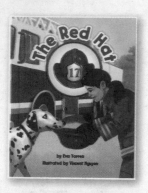

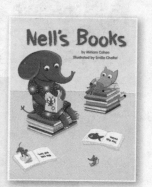

Changes Over Time

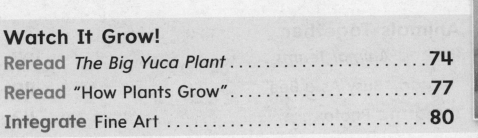

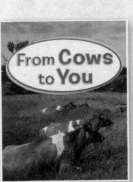

Animals Everywhere

Animal Features

Animals Together

In the Wild

Insects!

Working with Animals

Figure It Out

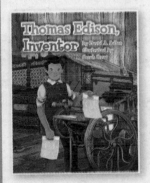

Together We Can!

(l) Steve Allen/Brand X Pictures; (cr signed language) George Ancona/McGraw-Hill Education; (r-brush) McGraw-Hill Education; (r-chessboard) Stockbyte/PunchStock

Nat and Sam

Literature Anthology: pages 6–17

? How do you know how Nat feels at school?

Talk About It Reread pages 8–9. What do you see Nat doing?

Text Evidence Write two things Nat is doing that help you see how he feels.

page 8	page 9

Write I can see that Nat feels

_____

- -

_____

Tip of the **Week**

Matt

When I **reread**, pictures help me understand.

? **How does the punctuation help you know how Nat feels?**

Talk About It Reread page 12. Talk about how the sentence shows how Nat is feeling.

Text Evidence Write how Nat feels in the top circle. Write two clues that help you know in the other circles.

Quick Tip

As I reread, I can use these sentence starters to talk about Nat.

I read that Nat...

The sentence shows...

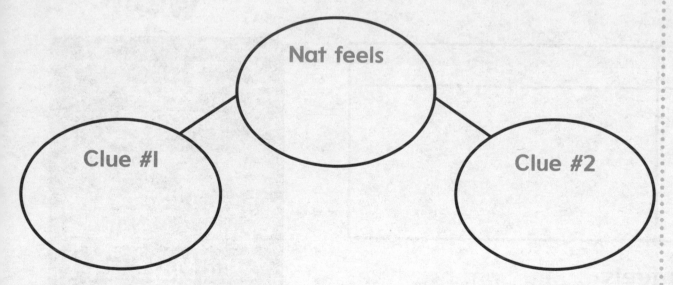

Nat feels

Clue #1

Clue #2

Write I know that Nat

_____

- - - - - - - - - - - - - - - - - - - -

_____

? **Why is the last sentence about Nat and Sam?**

COLLABORATE

Talk About It Reread pages 17. Talk about what Sam and Nat are doing. How does Nat feel now?

Text Evidence Write what Sam does and what Nat does. Write what they both do.

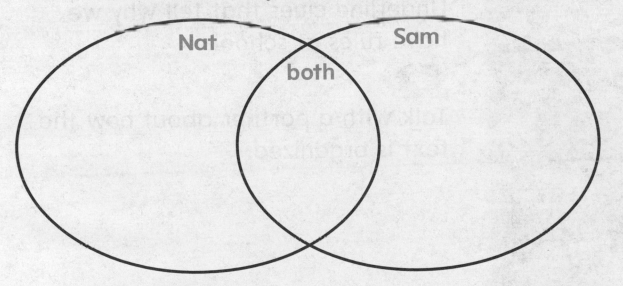

Nat

Sam

both

Write The sentence is about Nat and Sam because

_____

- -

_____

Your Turn

How do Nat's feelings about school change? Use these sentence starters:

I read that Nat feels...

I know his feelings change because...

Go Digital!
Write your response online.

Rules at School

Why do we have rules at school?

Rules can help us get along.

Rules can help us stay safe.

Reread and use the prompts to take notes in the text.

Draw a box around the clue that tells what the selection is about.

What is different about the first sentence? Circle the clue.

Underline clues that tell why we have rules at school.

COLLABORATE

Talk with a partner about how the text is organized.

Purestock/SuperStock

We raise our hands.

We listen quietly.

We obey safety rules.

We let everyone play!

What are your school rules?

Ariel Skelley/Blend Images/Getty Images

Underline ways to follow rules at school. Write two of them here.

_____

- -

_____

- -

_____

Which rule is different from the others? Draw a star next to it.

COLLABORATE

Look at the sentence with the star. Talk with a partner about how the rule is different.

? **How does "Rules at School" help you learn about rules?**

Talk About It Use your notes. Talk about ways the selection helps you learn about rules.

Text Evidence Write two clues that show how "Rules at School" helps you learn about rules.

A clue	How it helps me learn

Write "Rules at School" helps me learn by using

_____

- -

Quick Tip

I can find clues about how the selection helps me learn.

? **Why is the ABC song good to sing at school?**

COLLABORATE

Talk About It Talk about what Nat did at school and the rules you read about. Why do children learn the ABC song at school?

Text Evidence Put a star next to the clue that helps you know how the song helps children learn.

Write The ABC song is good to sing

_____

- -

_____

- -

_____

2HotBrazil/E+/Getty Images

CLOSE READING **Quick Tip**

I can tell about the song using these sentence starters:

The song is about...

Children sing it to...

ABC Song

A B C D E F G

H I J K L M N O P

Q R S T U V

W X Y and Z

Now I know my ABC's.

Next time won't you

sing with me?

Go, Pip!

? How do you know where the story takes place?

Literature Anthology: pages 26–39

Talk About It Reread pages 28–29. Where is Pip? How do you know?

Text Evidence Write three clues that help you know where Pip is.

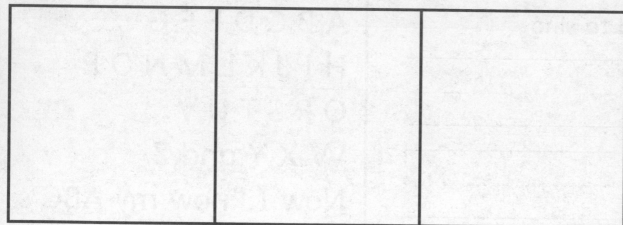

Write I know where Pip is because

_____

- -

_____

Tip
of the
Week

Sasha

I use clues in the illustrations when I reread.

wavebreakmedia/Shutterstock.com

? **How do you know Pip is not sure of his way around the city?**

COLLABORATE

Talk About It Reread pages 32–33. Talk about what Pip is doing.

Text Evidence Write clues from the words and illustrations that help you understand Pip's day in the city.

The text tells me	The illustrations show me

Write I know that Pip is not sure of his way around because

_____

- -

_____

CLOSE READING **Quick Tip**

As I reread, I can use sentence starters to talk about Pip.

The words tell me that Pip...

The illustrations show me that Pip...

 Why is *Go, Pip!* a good title for this story?

COLLABORATE

Talk About It Look at page 39. How is Pip feeling?

Text Evidence What clues help you know how Pip feels about his day? Write two clues here.

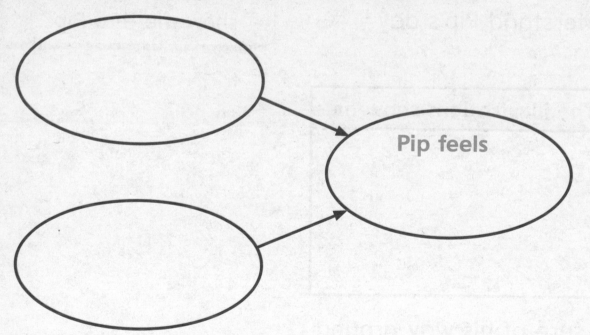

Pip feels

Write *Go Pip!* is a good title for this story because

_____

- -

_____

Your Turn

Describe how where Pip lives affects what he does. Use these sentence starters:

I read that Pip...

The words and illustrations help me know that Pip...

Go Digital!
Write your response online.

10   Unit I • Week 2 • Where I Live

I Live Here

I live in the **country**.

I live in a house.

Not many people live near us.

I live in the **city**.

I live in a big building.

Lots of people live here.

(t)Beau Lark/Corbis/VCG/Getty Images; (b)PhotoAlto/James Hardy/Getty Images

Reread and use the prompts to take notes in the text.

Circle two things about living in the country and two things about living in the city.

Draw a box around the words that repeat. Write them here.

_____

- - - - - - - - - - - - - - - - - - - -

_____

COLLABORATE

Talk with a partner about how the author compares two places. Draw pictures of the different places.

I live in the **country**.

I play in my yard.

Lots of kids play with me.

I live in the **city**.

I play in the playground.

Lots of kids play with me.

Circle two things about living in the country and two things about living in the city.

Compare them here.

Country	City
_____	_____
_____	_____
_____	_____
_____	_____

COLLABORATE

Talk with a partner about why the author makes some words darker than other words. Does it help you compare the places? Write **yes** or **no**.

? **Why does the author repeat the words "I live in" on every page?**

COLLABORATE

Talk About It Talk about where the people on each page live and what they do.

Text Evidence Use clues to tell what people do and see in the country and in the city.

country   both   city

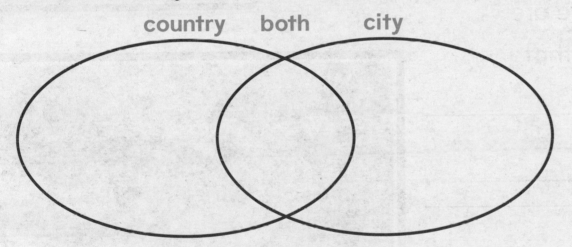

Write The author repeats "I live in" on every page because

_____

- - - - - - - - - - - - - - - - - - -

_____

Quick Tip

I can use the photographs to find clues about living in the country and in the city.

? **What can you tell about where these people are from the picture?**

Talk About It The illustrations in *Go, Pip!* tell about where Pip lives. What can you tell about where these people are from the picture?

Text Evidence Circle clues that help you understand where the people in the picture are.

Write The picture shows me that the people

_____

- -

_____

- -

_____

Read Together

Quick Tip

I can describe what parks are like using these sentence starters:

People go to the park to...

In the city...

People like to spend time in parks.

ImageZoo/SuperStock

Flip

? **How do Flip and the girl feel about being at school? How do you know?**

Literature Anthology: pages 48–61

Talk About It Reread pages 52–54. Talk about what is happening in the text and illustrations.

Text Evidence Find clues about how Flip and the girl feel when Flip goes to school.

Page	Text Clues	Picture Clues
52		
54		

Write The text and illustrations help me know that

_____

- -

_____

Tip of the Week

Marco

When I **reread**, I find clues about how the characters feel.

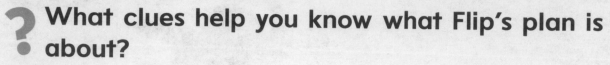

? **What clues help you know what Flip's plan is about?**

Talk About It Reread pages 58–59. Look at the illustrations and talk about what the teacher and Flip are doing.

Text Evidence Write three clues that help you know what Flip's plan is about.

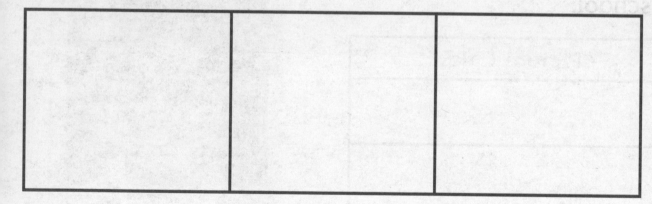

Write I can tell that Flip's plan is about

_____

- -

_____

? **What do you know about Flip that helps you imagine what the plan might be?**

Talk About It Reread pages 56–59. What do the illustrations show you about Flip?

Text Evidence Write three clues about Flip that can help you guess his plan.

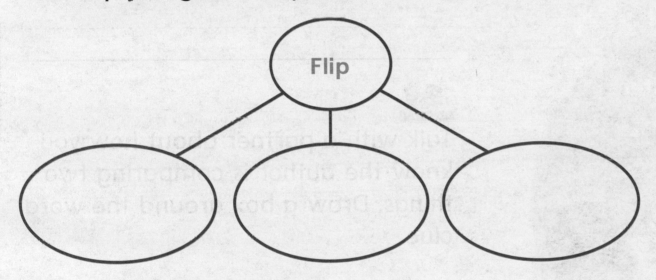

Flip

Write I imagine that Flip

_____

- - - - - - - - - - - - - - - - - - - -

_____

Read Together

Quick Tip

I can use story clues to help me know what a character is like. Then, I can imagine what might happen next.

Your Turn

Write a story about what happens when you take a make-believe pet to school. Use these sentence starters:

My make-believe pet is...

My pet is very...

Go Digital!
Write your response online.

What Pets Need

What do pets need?

Like all living things, pets need food.

Some pets eat seeds or plants.

hamster

Reread and use the prompts to take notes in the text.

What is different about the first sentence? Circle the clue.

What do pets need? Underline clues. Write them here.

_____

- -

_____

COLLABORATE

Talk with a partner about how you know the author is comparing two things. Draw a box around the word clue.

Juniors Bildarchiv/age fotostock

Some pets eat meat or fish.

All pets need fresh water.

Pets need a safe home.

Pets need our love
and care.

kittens

Lise Gagne/Vetta/Getty Images,

Underline four things pets need. Write them here.

_____ _____

_____ _____

_____ _____

_____ _____

COLLABORATE

Draw a box around the label. Talk about how labels help.

Circle what the label is naming.

? **Why is "What Pets Need" a good title for this selection?**

COLLABORATE

Talk About It Talk about the question on page 18.

Text Evidence Use clues to show how the author answers the question.

Talk about the question on page 18.

Page	What do pets need?

Write "What Pets Need" is a good title because

_____

- -

_____

Quick Tip
I can find clues to answer questions about the text.

? **How can you show that someone is special to you?**

COLLABORATE

Talk About It Talk about what made Flip a special pet. How did the girl show Flip that he was special to her?

Text Evidence Circle two examples of Owl telling Pussy that she is special to him.

Write You can show that someone is special by

_____

- -

_____

- -

_____

Quick Tip

I can describe how Owl feels using these sentence starters:

The Owl...

He tells Pussy-Cat...

from **The Owl and the Pussy-Cat**

The Owl looked up to the stars
   above,
And sang to a small guitar,
"O lovely Pussy! O Pussy, my love,
   What a beautiful Pussy you are."

— by Edward Lear

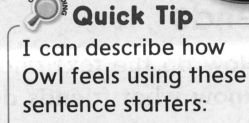

Friends

? How do the text and photographs help you know what friends do together?

COLLABORATE

Talk About It Reread pages 68–71. What do the friends do together?

Text Evidence Write clues from the text and photographs that help you know what friends can do.

Page 69	Page 70	Page 71

Write I know what friends can do because

_____

- -

_____

Read Together

Literature Anthology:
pages 68–81

CLOSE READING

Tip of the **Week**

Penny

When I **reread**, photographs help me understand the text.

MonkeyBusiness Images/Shutterstock.com

? **How do the photographs help show what Jill and Pam like and what they don't like?**

COLLABORATE

Talk About It Reread pages 72–75. Use the photographs to tell how the girls change.

Text Evidence Write what you know about Pam and Jill in the diagram.

Quick Tip

As I reread, I can use this sentence starter to talk about the friends.

I see that Jill and Pam...

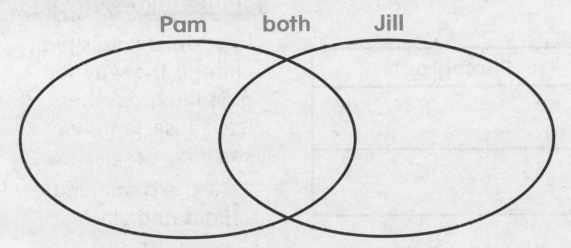

Pam   both   Jill

Write The photographs show me that

_____

- -

_____

? **How do you know Pam and Jill are good friends?**

COLLABORATE

Talk About It Reread pages 76–79. Why does Pam think of something else the friends can do?

Text Evidence What clues help you know that Pam is a good friend to Jill? Use the chart to record text evidence.

Page	Text	Photograph

Write Pam thinks of something else to do because

_____

- -

_____

Read Together

CLOSE READING **Quick Tip**

The photographs help me understand how the girls feel.

Your Turn

How does Pam's plan change the way the girls play together? Use these sentence starters:

At the beginning, Pam and Jill...

Pam's plan...

Go Digital!
Write your response online.

"There Are Days And There Are Days"

? How do the words in the poem help you know how the boy feels?

COLLABORATE

Talk About It Reread page 84. Which words help you understand how he feels when he is alone?

Text Evidence Write three clues from the text that help you understand how the boy feels when he isn't with a friend.

Write I can use words to understand

_____

- -

_____

Quick Tip

The poet uses rhyming words to tell me how the boy feels when he isn't with a friend.

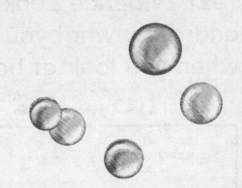

? **How does the illustration help you understand friends?**

COLLABORATE

Talk About It Look at the illustration on pages 84-85. How do you know the boys are friends?

Text Evidence Look at the illustration on one page and draw what you see. Then, draw what you see when you look at both pages together.

Quick Tip

As I reread, I can use these sentence starters to talk about the poem.

Friends can be....

When friends are together...

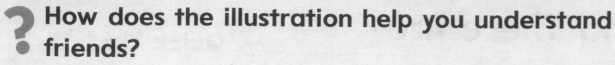

On one page	On both pages together

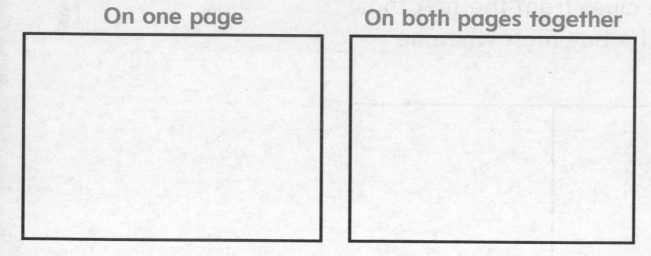

Write I see that friends

_____

- - - - - - - - - - - - - - - - - -

_____

? **How does the boy feel about spending time with a friend?**

COLLABORATE

Talk About It Reread the poem. What kinds of days are there?

Text Evidence Reread page 85. What words tell you the boy likes spending time with his friend? Write them here.

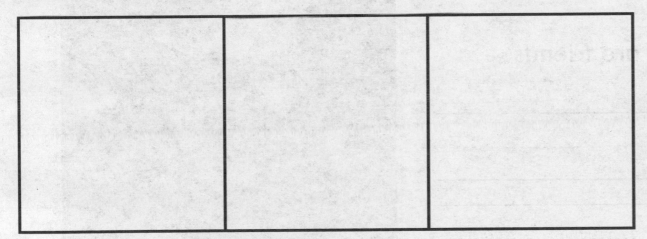

Write I know the boy feels

_____

- - - - - - - - - - - - - - - - - - - -

_____

I can find clues to understand a poem.

? How can you tell these children are friends?

COLLABORATE

Talk About It Talk about what the friends in the selections you read this week do and what the children in the painting are doing.

Text Evidence Circle clues that help you figure out that the children in the painting are friends.

Write I know the children are friends because

_____

- -

_____

- -

CLOSE READING Quick Tip

I can tell about the friends using these sentence starters:

The children...
They look...

Courtesy National Gallery of Art - Washington

The children play together.

Move It!

Literature Anthology:
pages 86–93

Read Together

? **How do the text and photographs help you understand how kids move?**

COLLABORATE

Talk About It Reread pages 88–89. Talk with a partner about what you see in the photographs.

Text Evidence Write clues that help you know how the children move.

	Text Clues	Photographs Clues
Jump		
Catch		

Write The children use their feet and hands to

_____

- -

_____

KidStock/Blend Images/Getty Images

CLOSE READING **Tip** of the **Week**

Rose

When I **reread**, the photographs tell more about the text.

? **How do the labels help you understand how the children swim and spin?**

COLLABORATE

Talk About It Reread pages 90–91. Why do you think the author uses those labels?

Text Evidence Find clues in the text and photographs to tell how each child moves.

What does the boy use to swim?	How does he move them?
What does the girl use to spin?	How does she move them?

Write The labels help me know

_____

- -

_____

CLOSE READING
Quick Tip

As I reread, I can use this sentence starter to talk about labels.

The labels help me find...

Your Turn

Describe the steps needed to make one of the motions in *Move It!* Use these sentence starters:

The text tells me ...

The photos show ...

This helps me know...

Go Digital!
Write your response online.

Using Diagrams

A diagram shows the different parts of something.

It is a picture with labels.

The labels name the parts.

fins

head

tail

gills

Don Farrall/Photodisc/Getty Images

Reread and use the prompts to take notes in the text.

Draw a box around the word that tells what this page is about.

Underline the clue that tells what a diagram does.

Add a label to the fish. Write it here.

_____

- - - - - - - - - - - - - - - - - - -

_____

COLLABORATE

Talk with a partner about how labels can be used to get more information.

? **What would be a good title for this diagram?**

COLLABORATE

Talk About It Reread "Using Diagrams." Talk about why the author chose the labels you see.

Text Evidence Find clues to tell what you learn from the text and from the diagram.

text	diagram

Write A good title would be

_____

- -

_____

CLOSE READING
Quick Tip
Labels can help me see what is the same and what is different.

? **How will these children move their bodies?**

COLLABORATE

Talk About It Discuss the ways to move that you read about this week. What does the caption say?

Text Evidence Draw labels on the photo for the body parts the children will use to play soccer. Circle the clue that helps you know one way the children will move.

Write The photo and caption help me know that

_____

- - - - - - - - - - - - - - - - - - - -

_____

_____

- - - - - - - - - - - - - - - - - - - -

_____

Kris Timken/Blend Images LLC

🔍 **Quick Tip**

I can explain the photo using these sentence starters:

The team is...

The children have...

The team is ready to kick around the soccer ball!

The Red Hat

 How do the illustrations help you know Jen's job is important?

Literature Anthology: pages 6–19

Talk About It Reread pages 10–11. Talk about what is happening in the illustrations. What is Jen doing on page 11?

Text Evidence Write clues from the illustrations that show what Jen has to do for her job.

 **Tip of the Week**

Clues on page 10	Clues on page 11

Eva

Write I know Jen's job is important because

_____

- -

_____

When I **reread**, I use clues from the illustrations to help me know important details.

? **Why does the author show Jen doing a different thing on each page?**

COLLABORATE

Talk About It Reread pages 15–16. Talk with a partner about what Jen does in the illustrations.

Text Evidence Use clues from the text and illustrations to write what Jen does on each page.

What does Jen do?

Page 15	Page 16

Write The author shows Jen doing different things

_____

_____

Quick Tip

As I reread, I can use these sentence starters to talk about what Jen does.

Jen can...

When the bell rings, Jen...

? **Why does the text say "Thank you, Jen!" after Jen gets Rex?**

COLLABORATE

Talk About It Reread page 19. Look at the illustrations. Who do you think is saying "thank you?"

Text Evidence Write clues from the text that help you know why Jim and Rex feel the way they do.

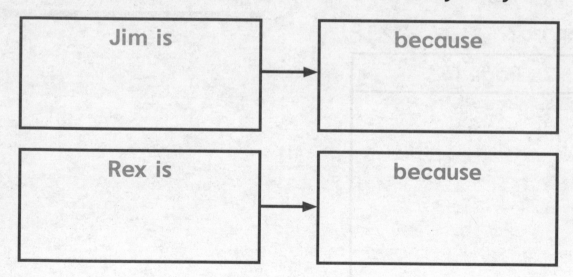

| Jim is | → | because |

| Rex is | → | because |

Write The text says "Thank you, Jen!" because

_____

_____

CLOSE READING
Quick Tip
I can use clues from the text to understand what I read.

Your Turn

Would you like to have Jen's job? Describe what you would like or not like, and why. Use these sentence starters:

I think Jen's job is...

I would like...

I would not like...

Go Digital!
Write your response online.

Firefighters at Work

A bell rings at the firehouse. Firefighters slide down a pole. They put on special clothes fast!

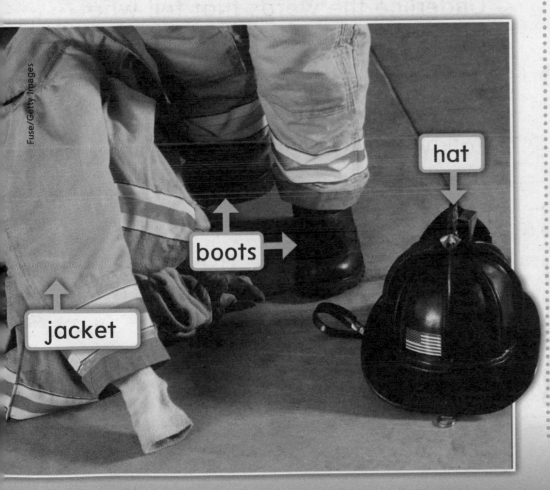

hat

boots

jacket

Fuse/Getty Images

Reread and use the prompts to take notes in the text.

Circle the words that tell how firefighters know it's time to go.

Underline two things the firefighters do next.

Put a star next to the word that tells how they put on special clothes.

Circle the labels for some of the special clothes. Write them here:

_____   _____

_____   _____

_____

The brave firefighters get to work.

They use hoses to spray water.

Their special clothes protect them.

They put out the fire!

What do the firefighters use to put out the fire? Circle the word.

How do the hoses help firefighters?

_____

_____

Underline the words that tell what the special clothes do.

COLLABORATE

Put a star on the word *brave*. Talk with a partner about why firefighters are brave.

Herve Donnezan/Age fotostock

? **How is the information in this selection organized?**

 COLLABORATE

Talk About It Reread the selection. What do you learn about firefighters on each page?

Text Evidence Use clues from the text and photos to tell what you learn first, next, then, and last.

Quick Tip

I can use the text and photographs to learn about jobs people do.

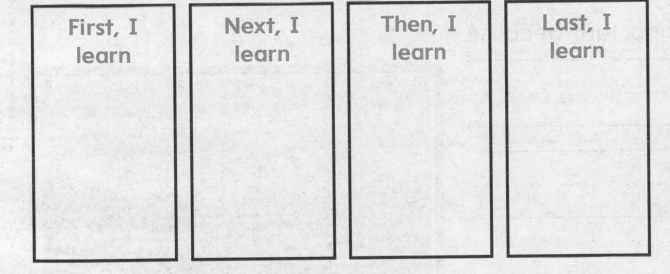

First, I learn	Next, I learn	Then, I learn	Last, I learn

Write The information tells me

_____

_____

? **How do you know the people in the painting are doing an important job?**

COLLABORATE

Talk About It Think about how firefighters' work helps a community. How does the work these people do help their community?

Text Evidence Circle the words that help you know their job is important.

Write I know the job is important because

_____

_____

_____

Quick Tip

I can explain the painting using these sentence starters:

The people are...

Wheat is...

image courtesy National Gallery of Art

These people are cutting wheat, an important food crop.

The Pigs, the Wolf, and the Mud

? How does the illustration show that the pigs' mud hut was a good place to live?

Literature Anthology: pages 26–41

Talk About It Reread pages 28–29. Talk about what the mud hut was like.

Text Evidence Write three reasons why the pigs' mud hut was good for them to live in.

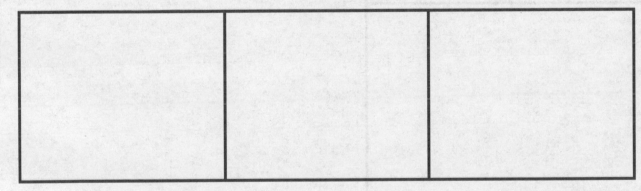

CLOSE READING

Tip of the Week

Write The hut was a good place for the pigs to live because

Luis

I use illustrations to know more about places and characters.

©KidStock/Blend Images/Corbis

? How do the pigs decide what they will use to build a new hut?

COLLABORATE

Talk About It Reread pages 40–41. Talk about what you see in the illustration.

Text Evidence Write clues from the text and illustration that tell you how the pigs decide.

Clues from the text	Clues from the illustration

Write The pigs decide to use mud

_____

- -

_____

CLOSE READING
Quick Tip
As I reread, I can use these sentence starters to talk about how the pigs decide.
  The wolf feels...
  They choose mud because...

? **How can you tell that the pigs' plan to build another mud hut is a good idea?**

COLLABORATE

Talk About It Reread page 41. Who likes the plan? Who does not?

Text Evidence Write clues from the dialogue that help you know who likes the plan and who does not.

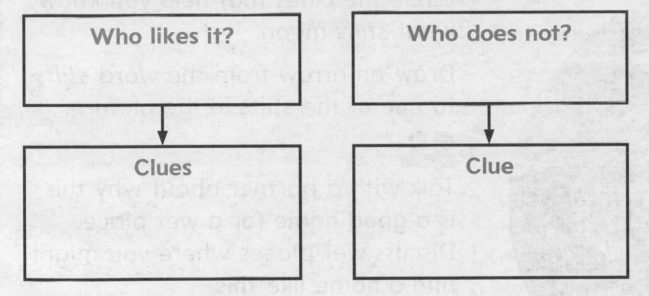

Who likes it?	Who does not?
↓	↓
Clues	Clue

Write A new mud hut is a good idea because

_____

- -

_____

Your Turn

The pigs need a plan. Write directions for the pigs to follow when they build their hut. Use these sentence starters:

First, the pigs need to...

Next, they can...

Then, they can...

Go Digital!
Write your response online.

Homes Around the World

This is a good home for a wet place. There is a lot of water here. The stilts help keep this home dry.

This home is made of wood.

Reread and use the prompts to take notes in the text.

Underline the word that tells what kind of place this is.

Draw a box around the word that tells what the home is made of.

Circle the clues that help you know what *stilts* mean.

Draw an arrow from the word *stilts* to one of the stilts in the picture.

COLLABORATE

Talk with a partner about why this is a good home for a wet place. Discuss wet places where you might find a home like this.

James Strachan/robertharding/Getty Images

This is a good home for a hot place. There is a lot of clay in this place. People use it to build homes. Clay keeps the home cool inside.

This home is made of clay.

Underline the word that tells what kind of place this is.

What is there a lot of in this place? Write the word here:

_____

_____

Underline the sentence that tells what people here do with clay.

COLLABORATE

Talk with a partner about where in the world this home might be. Use your notes and the picture for clues.

Sylvain Grandadam/The Image Bank/Getty Images

 Quick Tip
Captions tell me about what I see in the photographs.

? **Why is "Homes Around the World" a good title for this selection?**

COLLABORATE

Talk About It Reread the selection. Talk about what makes each home special.

Text Evidence Write how the homes on pages 44–45 are good homes for where they are.

Why is the home on page 44 a good home for a wet place?	
Why is the home on page 45 a good home for a hot place?	

Write "Homes Around the World" is a good title because

_____

- -

_____

? **How do you know that Old Joe Clark's house is special?**

COLLABORATE

Talk About It Talk about what the pigs' house was made of. What is Old Joe Clark's house full of? What does the word *story* mean in this song?

Text Evidence Circle two clues in the song that help you know Old Joe Clark's house is special.

Write Old Joe Clark's house is special because

_____

_____

_____

_____

CLOSE READING

Quick Tip

I can explain the song using these sentence starters:

  The house has...
  The house is full of...

Old Joe Clark

Old Joe Clark,
  he had a house,

Sixteen stories high.

And ev'ry story
  in that house

Was filled with
  chicken pie.

At a Pond

? How do the text and photographs help you understand what the selection is about?

Literature Anthology: pages 48–59

Read Together

COLLABORATE

Talk About It Reread pages 48–51. Talk about what it would be like to live at a pond.

Text Evidence Write the questions from the text. Write the answers you can find in the photographs.

Tip of the **Week**

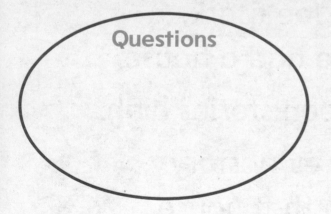

Questions

Answer

Write I know the selection is about

_____

- - - - - - - - - - - - - - - - - -

_____

Ben

When I reread, the questions help me know what it is about.

Alexandra Pavlova/Moment Open/Getty Images

? **Why does the author ask questions, but not answer them?**

COLLABORATE

Talk About It Reread page 55. Talk about the question and how you can find the answer.

Text Evidence Write one clue from the text and from the photo that help you answer the question.

CLOSE READING
Quick Tip

I can use sentence starters to talk about the ducks.

Ducks make nests out of...

The eggs in the nest...

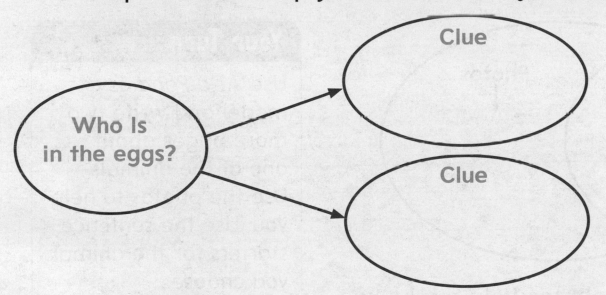

Who Is in the eggs?

Clue

Clue

Write The author asks questions in the text, so

_____

- -

_____

? How does the information on these pages help you know who lives at a pond?

Talk About It Reread pages 56–57. Talk about the details you can find about who lives at a pond.

Text Evidence Write what the photos tell you and what the text tells you. What details are in both?

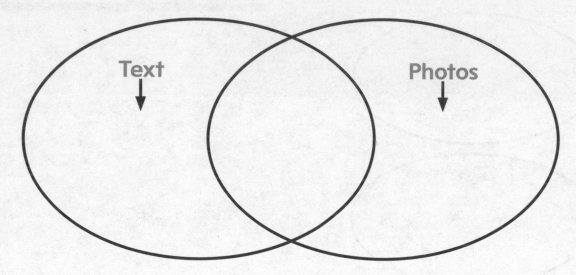

Text

Photos

Write Details in the text and photos help me know

Quick Tip

When I reread, I can use clues from the text and photographs to answer questions.

Your Turn

Use *At a Pond* as a model and write two more pages about one of the animals. Use the photos to help you. Use the sentence starters for the animal you choose:

Frogs live...

They can...

Go Digital!
Write your response online.

Way Down Deep

? What place is this poem about?

COLLABORATE

Talk About It Reread pages 62–63. Find the words that repeat. What do they tell you?

Text Evidence Write clues from the illustration and text that tell you what place the poem is about.

The text says...   The illustration shows...

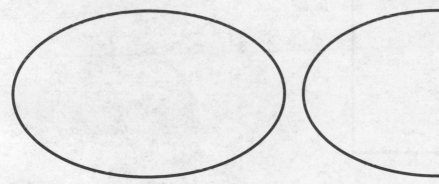

Write The illustration and text tell me the place is

_____

- -

_____

Quick Tip

CLOSE READING

When a poem is about a place, I can find clues that help me know where.

? **How does the author help you know how the animals in the poem move?**

COLLABORATE

Talk About It Reread pages 62–63. How does the illustration help you understand the poem?

Text Evidence Write words that help you know how the animals move.

Quick Tip
CLOSE READING

I can use these sentence starters to talk about how the animals move.

Underneath the ocean...

Starfish and snails...

Oysters...

Write The animals in the poem

_____

_____

_____

How does the poem help you know what the bottom of the ocean is like?

Talk About It Reread pages 62–63. What does the illustration show you about the bottom of the ocean?

Text Evidence Use clues from the text to fill in the chart.

 Quick Tip
I can use clues to know what a place is like.

The Bottom of the Ocean

Where is it?	What is there?	What do animals do?

Write The poem helps me know that the bottom of the ocean is

_____

- -

_____

? **How is a forest a different kind of home for animals than water?**

COLLABORATE

Talk About It Talk about how the forest in the painting is different from the ocean and pond you read about.

Text Evidence Circle clues in the painting and caption that help you know what kind of home a forest is.

Write A forest is a different kind of home because

_____

- - - - - - - - - - - - - - - - - - - -

_____

- - - - - - - - - - - - - - - - - - - -

_____

Yale University Art Gallery

Birds build a nest high in a tree.

Nell's Books

Literature Anthology: pages 64–79

? What do the text and illustration tell you about Nell?

COLLABORATE

Talk About It Reread pages 66–67. Talk about what you see in the illustration.

Text Evidence Write three things you know about Nell. Tell where you found clues to help you know.

I know that Nell...	I found a clue in the...

Write The text and illustration tell me that Nell

_____

- -

_____

CLOSE READING

Tip of the Week

Robert

When I reread, I can find details in the illustrations.

Jupiterimages/Fbdand/Getty Images Plus/Getty Images

? **How do the illustrations help you know how Nell and her friends feel?**

COLLABORATE

Talk About It Reread pages 72–75. Talk about what is happening in the illustrations.

Text Evidence Write clues from the illustrations that tell you how the characters feel.

Quick Tip

I can use these sentence starters to talk about how Nell helps her friends.

Nell helps her friends by…

Her friends learn…

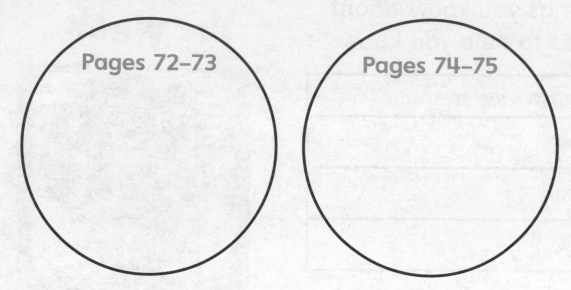

Pages 72–73

Pages 74–75

Write The illustrations help me know that

_____

- -

_____

? How does the dialogue help you know why Nell's friends made a bookmobile?

COLLABORATE

Talk About It Reread pages 76–77. What do Nell's friends say?

Text Evidence Write clues from the dialogue that tell why Nell's friends made a bookmobile.

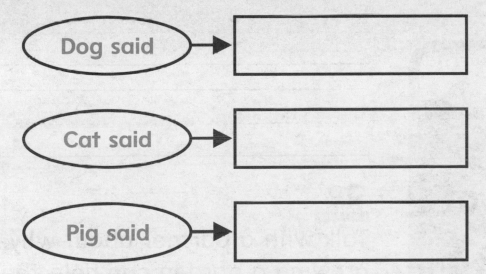

Dog said →

Cat said →

Pig said →

Write The dialogue helps me know why because

_____

- -

_____

CLOSE READING

Quick Tip

I can learn why characters do things from what they say.

Your Turn

Use *Nell's Books* as a model to write a fantasy about a character who helps.

Use these sentence starters:

My character likes to...

My character helps when...

Go Digital!
Write your response online.

Kids Can Help!

How can kids help the neighborhood? Kids can help grow a garden! It is fun to plant seeds and help them grow.

Reread and use the prompts to take notes in the text.

Circle the question.

Underline the answer.

Write two things kids can do in the garden.

_____

_____

_____

_____

COLLABORATE

Talk with a partner about why growing a garden can help the neighborhood.

Norma Jean Gargasz/Alamy Stock Photo

Kids can help clean the playground. They can pick up trash. They can recycle cans and bottles.

Recycling makes the neighborhood clean. Recycling helps our Earth, too.

Underline the sentence that tells another place where kids can help.

Write two things kids can do to help.

_____

_____

_____

_____

Circle how recycling helps the neighborhood.

COLLABORATE

Talk with a partner about the ways recycling helps.

? Why is "Kids Can Help!" a good title?

COLLABORATE

Talk About It Talk about some ways to help your neighborhood in "Kids Can Help!"

Text Evidence Use clues from your notes to write about the ideas in "Kids Can Help!"

Quick Tip
I can use the title to help me know what the text is about.

Kids can help grow a garden.	Kids can help clean the playground.
They can	They can
They can	They can

Write "Kids Can Help!" is a good title because

_____

_____

? **How does Little Boy Blue help when he's awake?**

COLLABORATE

Talk About It Talk about how kids can help their community. How did Nell help others?

Text Evidence Circle two clues that help you know what Little Boy Blue's job is.

Write Little Boy Blue helps when he

_____

- -

_____

- -

_____

CLOSE READING **Quick Tip**

I can describe how he helps using the sentence starters:

Little Boy Blue helps by...

Other kids help by...

Little Boy Blue

Little boy blue, come blow
    your horn;

The sheep's in the meadow,
    the cow's in the corn.

Where is the boy who looks
    after the sheep?

He's under the haystack,
    fast asleep.

Fun with Maps

? How do the maps' titles help you know what they show?

Talk About It Reread pages 87–89. Talk about the titles on the maps and the places the maps show.

Text Evidence Use clues from the maps to write what you see in each.

Map	What You See	What kind of Place
Phil's Room		
Town of Chatwell		

Write The titles of maps can

_____

- - - - - - - - - - - - - - - - - - - -

_____

Literature Anthology:
pages 86–93

Tip of the Week

CLOSE READING

Maria

When I **reread**, I look at the map to know the places it shows.

Tetra Images/Getty Images

? **How does the map's key help you understand more about the map?**

 COLLABORATE

Talk About It Reread pages 90–91. Talk about what you see in the map key. Do you see those things anywhere else on the page?

Text Evidence Use the map key to write what is on the map. Write or draw places and things you see.

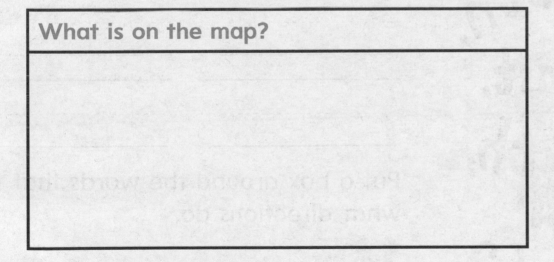

What is on the map?

Write The map key helps me know

_____

_____

CLOSE READING

Quick Tip

As I reread, I can use these sentence starters to talk about maps:

Some maps...

A map key shows...

Your Turn

Why does the author show different kinds of maps? What does this help us understand about maps? Use these sentence starters:

The author wants to...

This helps show...

Go Digital!
Write your response online.

North, East, South, or West?

Many maps show directions. North, East, South, and West are directions. Directions tell us which way to go.

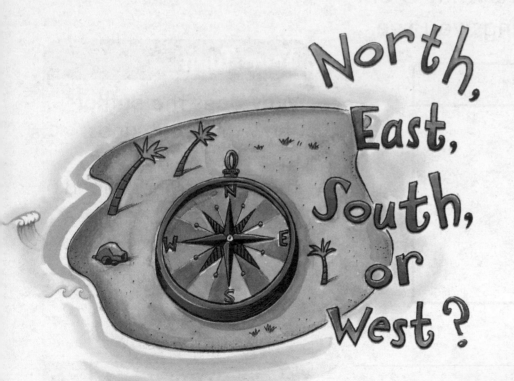

North, East, South, or West?

Reread and use the prompts to take notes in the text.

Circle the word that tells what many maps show.

Underline the words that tell what directions are.

Write the words here:

_____   _____

_____   _____

_____   _____

Put a box around the words that tell what directions do.

COLLABORATE

Talk with a partner about directions and what you think the letters on the compass stand for.

Circle the map key.

Circle where North is on the map.

Put a box around the animal that is closest to East.

Put a triangle around the animal that is closest to South.

Talk with a partner about whether the chairs are north or south of the snack bar.

Illustration: Steven Mach

Key
N = North
E = East
S = South
W = West

? **How are maps of stars and maps of towns the same?**

COLLABORATE

Talk About It Talk with a partner about clues in the caption and in the map that help you know more about maps of stars.

Text Evidence Circle clues that help you figure out how maps of stars and maps of towns are the same.

Write Maps of stars and maps of towns both show

_____

- -

_____

- -

_____

Quick Tip

I can compare using these sentence starters:

Both maps show...
Maps of stars are different because...

McGraw-Hill Education

In this star map, the dots show where stars are located. Lines show pictures that people imagine to remember groups of stars. Words tell their names.

On My Way to School

? **How do you know who is telling the story?**

COLLABORATE

Literature Anthology: pages 6–21

Talk About It Reread pages 10–11. Talk about what is happening in the story.

Text Evidence Write two clues that help you know who tells the story.

CLOSE READING

Tip of the Week

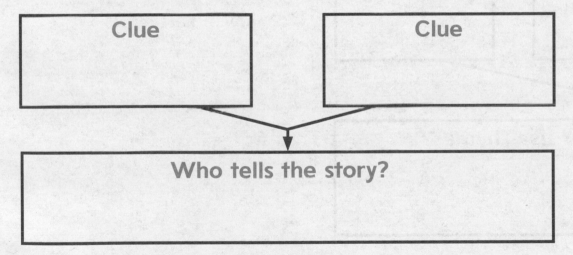

Clue	Clue

Who tells the story?

Luke

When I reread, I find clues in the text about who is telling the story.

Write Text and illustrations give me clues to know that

_____

- -

_____

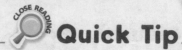

? **Why do you think the author chose to write this story with rhymes?**

COLLABORATE

Talk About It Reread pages 11–13. Are the sentences with rhymes more fun to read quietly or aloud?

Text Evidence Write pairs of rhyming words in the chart. Write why you think the author used them.

🔍 **Quick Tip**

As I reread, I can use sentence starters to talk about stories that rhyme:

Rhymes can...

When a story has rhymes...

Page 11

Page 12

Page 13

Why does the author use rhymes?

Write The author uses rhyming words

_____

- - - - - - - - - - - - - - - - - - - -

_____

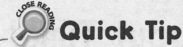

? **Why do you think the author had such strange things happen to make the boy late?**

Talk About It Reread pages 18–21. Talk about what happens in the story. What is odd?

Text Evidence Write about three things on these pages that could not happen in real life.

What Happens	Why It Could Not Happen In Real Life

Write Strange things happen in the story because

_____

- -

Your Turn

Write four more pages of the story. Tell the excuses the boy might give his mom for getting home late. Try these sentence starters:

When the bell rang after school...

Next, I saw a...

Go Digital!
Write your response online.

It's About Time!

Some clocks have faces with hands. The hands point to the numbers. Some clocks have just numbers.

All clocks tell the hour and minute. There are 60 minutes in an hour. There are 60 seconds in a minute.

Reread and use the prompts to take notes in the text.

Underline the sentence that says what all clocks tell.

How are the first three lines different from the last three lines?

How many seconds are in a minute? Write the answer here:

_____

- - - - - - - - - - - - - - - - - -

_____

COLLABORATE

Talk with a partner about how clocks are different. Draw a box around the clues.

(t)McGraw-Hill Education; (b)Stockbyte/Getty Images

Long ago, people didn't have clocks. They used the sun to tell time instead. Tools like sundials helped them. The sun's shadow showed the hour. But people had to guess the minutes. What time is this sundial showing?

David J. Green/Alamy

Underline the words that tell how people told time long ago.

Underline the sentence that tells what tool people used before clocks.

Circle the part of the photograph that shows the hour.

COLLABORATE

Talk with a partner about what time the sundial shows. How do you know?

? **Why did the author write "It's About Time!"?**

COLLABORATE

Talk About It Reread the selection. Talk about the information on each page.

Text Evidence Find two clues from the text that help explain why the author wrote this selection.

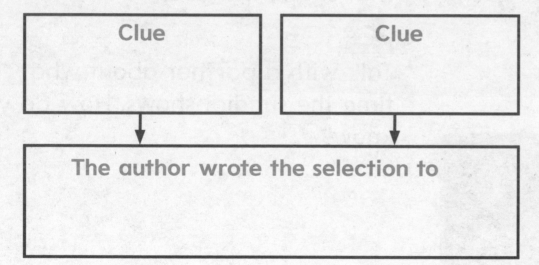

Clue	Clue

The author wrote the selection to

Write The author wrote the selection to tell about

_____

- - - - - - - - - - - - - - - - - - - -

_____

Quick Tip

I can use clues from the text and illustrations to know why the author wrote the selection.

Read Together

? **What kinds of things do we do in the morning?**

CLOSE READING **Quick Tip**

I can compare the texts using these sentence starters:

Both texts start with...

The poem is also about...

Talk About It Talk about how the poem is similar to the beginning of *On My Way to School* and "It's About Time."

Text Evidence Circle two clues from the poem that help you know what time of day it is.

Write In the morning we

_____

- -

_____

- -

_____

Time to Rise

A birdie with a yellow bill
Hopped upon my window sill,
Cocked his shining eye and said:
"Ain't you 'shamed, you
sleepy-head!"

— Robert Louis Stevenson

The Big Yuca Plant

Read Together

Literature Anthology:
pages 28–43

? **What do exclamation points tell you about how characters feel?**

COLLABORATE

Talk About It Reread pages 32–33. Talk about how the exclamation points show characters' feelings.

Text Evidence Write the sentences with exclamation points. Then write how the character feels.

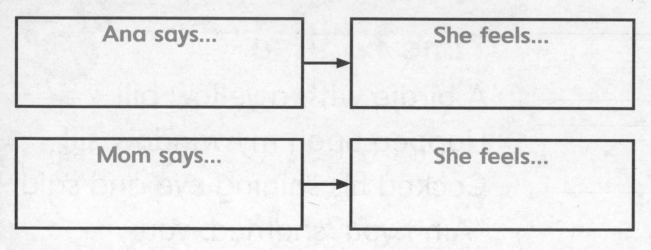

| Ana says... | → | She feels... |
| Mom says... | → | She feels... |

Write Exclamation points tell me the characters feel

_____

- -

_____

CLOSE READING **Tip of the Week**

Eliza

When I reread, exclamation points tell me a character has a strong feeling.

? **What do you learn about Lola from the way she plants and pulls out the yuca?**

COLLABORATE

Talk About It Reread pages 32 and 36. What does Lola do when she plants and pulls the yuca? Who does she work with?

Text Evidence Write how Lola works with others to plant and pull the yuca. Then write what this tells you about her.

How Lola plants and pulls the yuca	What this tells you about Lola

Write When Lola works with others, it shows

_____

- -

Quick Tip
CLOSE READING

As I reread, I can use sentence starters to talk about what the characters do and feel:

Lola lets...

Lola likes...

? **How does the dialogue help you learn about the characters?**

Talk About It Reread pages 40–41. What does each character say?

Text Evidence Write how what each character says tells you about him or her.

When...	it helps me know...
Lola says:	
Paco says:	
Rat says:	

Write The dialogue helps me learn _____

Your Turn

What else might Rat say? Write more lines for Rat to say at the end of the play. Use these sentence starters:

I am glad that...

I am wise, but...

Small helpers can...

Go Digital!
Write your response online.

How Plants Grow

When the seed is planted, a root grows down in the soil. The root holds the seed in the soil. It takes in water, too.

The stem grows up from the seed. When it pops out of the soil, it is called a sprout. Green leaves grow on the stem.

Nic Miller/Organics image library/Alamy

Reread and use the prompts to take notes in the text.

Underline what happens after the seed is planted.

Circle what the root does.

Underline the word that tells what grows up.

On the photograph circle what grows next.

COLLABORATE

Talk with a partner about what a sprout is. Make a label pointing to the sprout in the photograph.

Over time, blossoms pop up on the plant. These blossoms are the plant's flowers. They can grow into a fruit such as this pumpkin. Many fruits can grow on one plant vine.

Inside the fruit are seeds. These seeds can be used to grow new plants.

fruit

blossom

Circle the word that tells what blossoms are.

Underline the words that tell what flowers do.

Draw a box around the word that tells what is inside a fruit. Write the word here.

_____

- -

_____

COLLABORATE

Talk with a partner about what will happen to the blossom in the picture.

? **How does the author organize the information in this selection?**

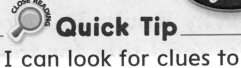
Quick Tip

I can look for clues to help me see the order that events happen.

COLLABORATE

Talk About It Reread "How Plants Grow." Talk about how the details are organized.

Text Evidence Write what you learn from the selection first, next, then, and last.

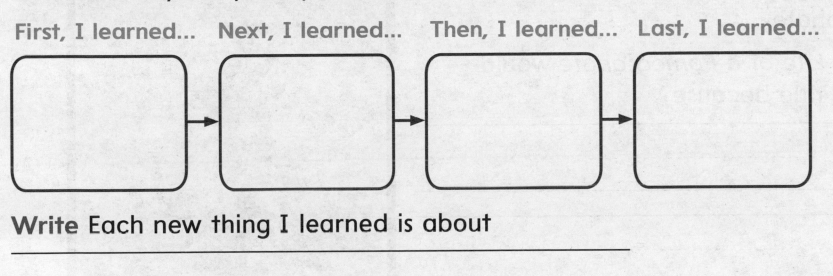

First, I learned...   Next, I learned...   Then, I learned...   Last, I learned...

Write Each new thing I learned is about

_____

_____

? **Why would *The Life of a Pomegranate* be a good title for this painting?**

Talk About It How does a pomegranate grow like the other plants you read about this week?

Text Evidence Circle clues from the painting and the text that show it is about the life of a pomegranate.

Write *The Life of a Pomegranate* would be a good title because

_____

_____

_____

Quick Tip

I can describe how fruit grows using these sentence starters:

First a seed...
Then the plant...

This painting shows pomegranate seeds, tree, blossoms, and fruit.

80   Unit 3 • Week 2 • Watch It Grow!

The Gingerbread Man

Read Together

? Why do you think the author repeats words in the story?

Literature Anthology: pages 50–65

COLLABORATE

Talk About It Reread pages 56–57. Talk about which words repeat. How do the repeating words give the story rhythm?

CLOSE READING **Tip** of the **Week**

Text Evidence Write the sentences with the repeating words.

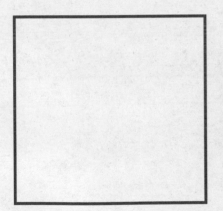

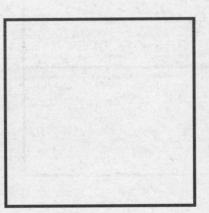

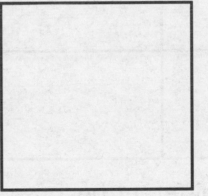

Anna

Write Repeating words make a sentence

_____

- - - - - - - - - - - - - - - - - - -

_____

When I **reread**, I use the repeating words to help me read aloud.

Sam74100/iStock/360/Getty Images

? **What is different when the Gingerbread Man meets the fox?**

COLLABORATE

Talk About It Reread pages 58–61. What happens when the Gingerbread Man meets the duck? What happens when he meets the fox?

Text Evidence Use clues from the text to fill in the chart.

Quick Tip

I can use clues to know when something different happens in a story.

What does the duck do? Is it the *same* or *different* from what happens before?	What does the fox do? Is it the *same* or *different* from what happens before?

Write Meeting the fox is different because

_____

_____

? **How do the illustrations help you understand what is happening?**

Talk About It Reread pages 63–65. What are the Gingerbread Man and the fox doing? How do the pictures help you know what the fox is doing?

Text Evidence Write what you see in each picture.

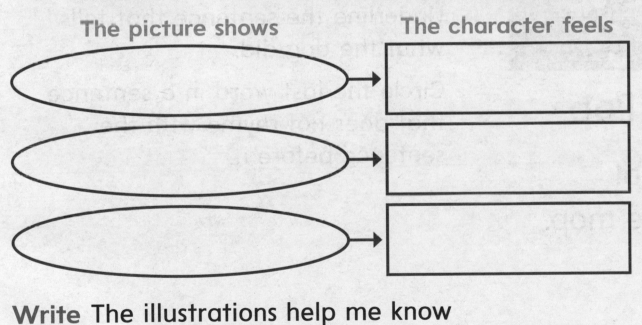

The picture shows → The character feels

Write The illustrations help me know

_____

Quick Tip

I can look at the illustrations for clues about what happens in the story.

Your Turn

Imagine that the Gingerbread Man decided to run around the lake. Write a new ending to the story. Use these sentence frames:

The Gingerbread Man said...

Then the Gingerbread Man...

Go Digital!
Write your response online.

Mother Goose Rhymes

Higglety, Pigglety Pop

Higglety, pigglety, pop!

The dog has eaten the mop.

The pig's in a hurry.

The cat's in a flurry.

Higglety, pigglety, pop!

Reread and use the prompts to take notes in the text.

Circle the word that rhymes with *pop.* Write the word.

_____

- -

_____

Underline the sentence that tells what the dog did.

Circle the last word in a sentence that does not rhyme with the sentence before it.

Hey! Diddle, Diddle

Hey! diddle, diddle,

The cat and the fiddle,

The cow jumped over the moon;

The little dog laughed

To see such sport,

And the dish ran away with

the spoon.

Circle the word that rhymes with *moon*. Write the word.

_____

- - - - - - - - - - - - - - - -

_____

Underline the words that tell what the cow did.

Underline the words that tell what the dog did.

COLLABORATE

Talk with a partner about what it would look like if a dish ran away with a spoon.

? **What do the rhyming words do for the poems?**

COLLABORATE

Talk About It Reread the selection. Talk about the poems. Are they easy or hard to remember? Are they fun to say?

Text Evidence Write the rhyming words from each poem.

Quick Tip
I can look for rhyming words when I read a poem.

page 84	page 84

page 85	page 85

Write The rhyming words make the poems

_____

- - - - - - - - - - - - - - - - - - -

_____

? How do folktales use made-up characters to help you learn?

COLLABORATE

Talk About It Talk about the folktales you read this week. What kinds of characters are in *The Gingerbread Man*?

Text Evidence Circle clues from the illustration and the caption that help you know what the story is about.

Write Folktales use made-up characters to

_____

_____

_____

_____

©Ivy Close Images/Alamy

Quick Tip

I can describe the story using these sentence starters:

The tortoise and the hare are...

The story teaches...

This illustration shows a folktale about a race. The tortoise beat the hare. "Slow and steady wins the race," said the tortoise.

Long Ago and Now

? Why does the author ask and answer a question in the first paragraph?

Literature Anthology: pages 74–87

 **Read Together**

Talk About It Reread page 76. Talk about the question and answer in the first paragraph.

Text Evidence Write what the answer helps you know.

 **Tip of the Week**

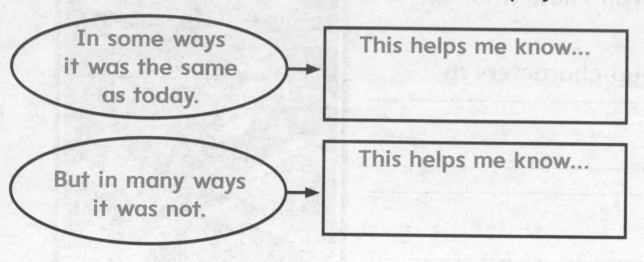

In some ways it was the same as today. → This helps me know...

But in many ways it was not. → This helps me know...

Write The question and answer helps me know

_____

- - - - - - - - - - - - - - - - - - -

Mateo

When I **reread**, I look at how the author gives information.

? **How do the photographs help you understand the information in the text?**

COLLABORATE

Talk About It Reread pages 78–79. Talk about what you see in the photographs.

Text Evidence Use clues from the text to write what the photographs show.

Quick Tip
I can use photographs to see things I read about in the text.

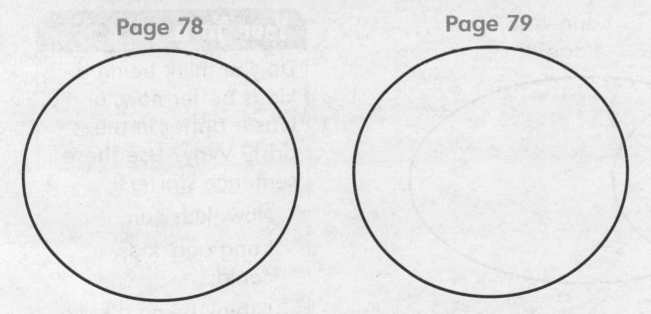

Page 78

Page 79

Write Photographs can help me when they show

_____

- -

_____

**Read Together**

? How does the author organize the information on these pages? Why?

Talk About It Reread pages 80–81. Discuss what each page is about.

Text Evidence Write what you learned from the text and the photographs on these pages.

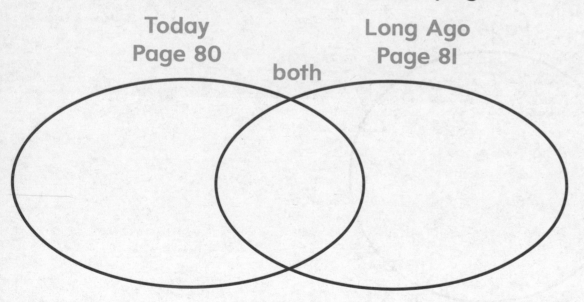

Today
Page 80

both

Long Ago
Page 81

Write The author organizes information to help me

_____

- -

_____

Quick Tip

I use details to help compare today with long ago.

Your Turn

Do you think being a kid is better now, or was it better in the past? Why? Use these sentence starters:

Now, kids can...

Long ago, kids could...

I think being a kid is better...

Go Digital!
Write your response online.

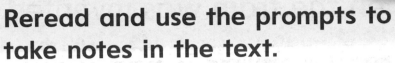

From Horse to Plane

People today can go places in cars, planes, and trains. Long ago there were not as many kinds of transportation. Before engines, people had to walk or use horses.

Library of Congress Prints and Photographs Division (LC-D41-891)

Reread and use the prompts to take notes in the text.

Underline the words that tell how we can go places today.

Write the words that tell how people went places long ago:

_____

_____

_____

_____

COLLABORATE

Talk with a partner about details the photograph shows that you did not read about in the text.

Then the train was invented. Steam engines made them go. Now people could go places much faster. It used to take days to go a hundred miles. After the train was invented, it might take hours.

Circle the word that tells what this page is about.

Draw a box around the words that tell what made trains go.

Write the words here:

_____

- -

_____

Underline the sentence that tells what trains helped people do.

COLLABORATE

Talk with a partner about what it was like to travel before the train was invented.

? How does the title "From Horse to Plane" help you understand what the selection is about?

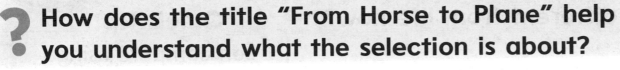

Read Together

Quick Tip
I can use the title to know what the selection is about.

Talk About It Talk about the information on each page.

Text Evidence Use clues from the text to write how people changed how they went places.

First	Next	Last

Write The title tells me

_____

- - - - - - - - - - - - - - - - - - -

_____

? **How is life in the song different from life now?**

COLLABORATE

Talk About It Reread the song. Talk about what you learned about how people got around using horses in "From Horse to Plane." How will the narrator in the poem use the pony?

Text Evidence Circle clues that show how the narrator will use the pony.

Write Life in the song is different than now because

_____

- -

_____

- -

_____

CLOSE READING **Quick Tip**

I can compare using these sentence starters:

In the song...

Now people...

Caballito Blanco
(Little White Pony)

Caballito blanco,

Take me far away.

Take me to my birthplace,

Where I want to stay.

Photo 24/age fotostock

From Cows to You

? **How do the photographs help you understand the information?**

Literature Anthology:
pages 94–101

COLLABORATE

Talk About It Reread pages 96–97. Talk about what you see in the photographs.

Text Evidence Write what the text says.

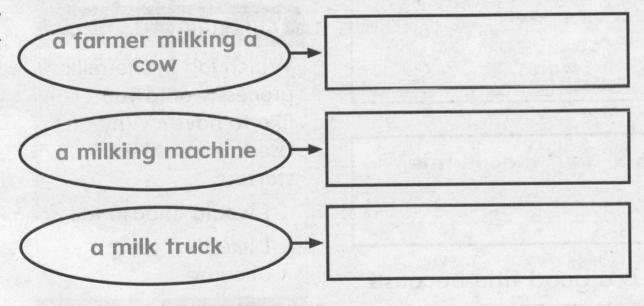

(a farmer milking a cow) →

(a milking machine) →

(a milk truck) →

Westend61/Getty Images

Write Photographs show me

_____

- -

_____

CLOSE READING **Tip of the Week**

Lisa

When I reread, I use photographs to understand the text.

? Why is "From Cows to You" a good title for this selection?

COLLABORATE

Talk About It Reread pages 96–99. Discuss why the title goes with the text.

Text Evidence Use details to tell what the selection is about. Tell why "From Cows to You" is a good title.

What is this selection about?

↓

Why is "From Cows to You" a good title?

Write "From Cows to You" is a good title because

_____

- -

_____

Read Together

CLOSE READING
Quick Tip
When I reread, I can pay attention to what the title means.

Your Turn

Which job in the milk process would you like to have? Why? Use these sentence starters:

I would choose to...

I like that job because...

Go Digital!
Write your response online.

Read Together

A Food Chart

Dairy is one food group. The other food groups are grains, fruits, vegetables, and protein. A healthy diet must have food from every group.

JGI/Jamie Grill/Blend Images/Getty Images

Reread and use the prompts to take notes in the text.

Circle the words that tell the five food groups.

Write the words here:

_____   _____

_____   _____

_____   _____

_____   _____

_____

_____

Underline the sentence that tells what a healthy diet has.

Draw a box around the food group the boy is drinking.

? **Why does the author include the food group chart?**

COLLABORATE

Talk About It Reread pages 102–103. Talk about what the chart teaches you that the text does not.

Text Evidence List reasons why a chart might be a better way to share certain information.

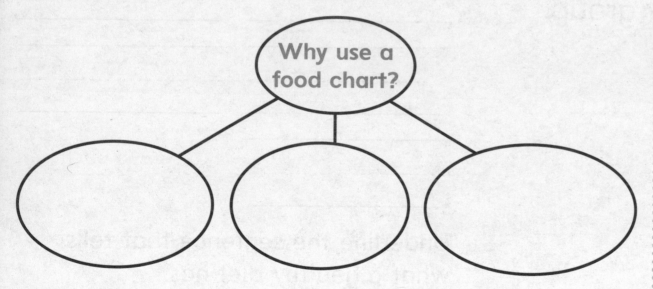

Why use a food chart?

Write The author uses the chart because

_____

- -

_____

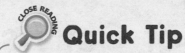

? What does the painting help you learn about where olives come from?

Talk About It Talk about where the milk comes from in *From Cow to You*. How is getting milk like getting olives?

Text Evidence Circle clues in the painting and caption that help you know where olives come from.

Write The food we eat comes from

_____

- -

_____

_____

- -

_____

Courtesy National Gallery of Art - Washington

Quick Tip

I can describe what happens using these sentence starters:

   In *From Cow to You*, the milk...
   Olives also...

Read Together

CLOSE READING

This painting shows workers picking olives.

How Bat Got Its Wings

Literature Anthology: pages 10–27

Read Together

COLLABORATE

? What clues help you know what Gray Bat is like at the beginning of the story?

Talk About It Reread page 17. What words does the author use to describe Gray Bat?

Text Evidence Write three clues from the text and illustration that help you know what Gray Bat looks like.

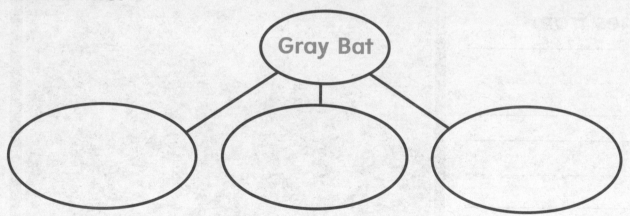

Gray Bat

Write I learned that Gray Bat _____

_____

- -

_____

CLOSE READING

Tip of the **Week**

Ana

When I reread, I use illustrations to help me find clues about a character.

Image Source/Vetta/Getty Images

? **How does the dialogue help you know how the birds will help Gray Bat?**

COLLABORATE

Talk About It Reread page 20. Talk about how the birds feel about Gray Bat.

Text Evidence Write what you learned from the dialogue about how the birds will solve the problem.

Quick Tip

As I reread, I can use these sentence starters to talk about Gray Bat.

Gray Bat can't...

The birds will help Gray Bat by...

Problem		Solution
	→	

Write The dialogue helps me know that the birds

_____

- -

_____

? How do the illustrations help you understand how Gray Bat changed?

COLLABORATE

Talk About It Reread pages 22–25. Talk about what Gray Bat looks like now.

Text Evidence Write what you learned about how Gray Bat *is* and *is not* like the birds.

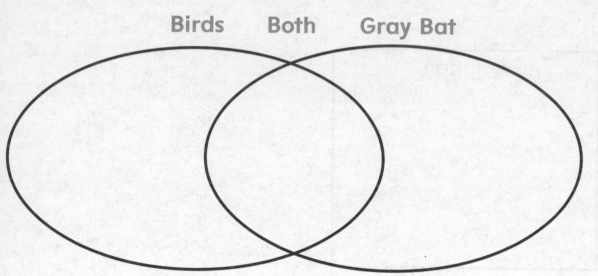

Birds   Both   Gray Bat

Write The illustrations show me that now Gray Bat

_____

- -

_____

Quick Tip
CLOSE READING
When I reread, I can use illustrations to help me compare what is the same and different.

Your Turn

Bat flies in his own way with his own special wings. Write a folktale explaining how an animal got a special body part. Use sentence starters like these:

At first, my animal...

Then, my animal gets...

The special body part helps...

Go Digital!
Write your response online.

Bats! Bats! Bats!

Bat or Bird?

Body Part	Bat	Bird
Ears	Big ears to hear at night	No big ears, but has small holes on side of head
Covering	Fur (hair)	Feathers
Wings	Two wings made of thin skin and hair; four fingers and a thumb on each wing	Two wings with feathers
Legs	Two short legs with claws	Two long legs with claws
Nose	Big nose that comes in many shapes and sizes	No nose, but has a bill, or beak

A bat is the only mammal that can fly. But it is not a bird.

Look at the chart. It tells the ways a bat and a bird are the same and different.

Reread and use the prompts to take notes in the text.

Put a star next to the sentence that tells what the chart does.

Write the names of the two animals that the chart compares.

_____   _____

_____   _____

Underline the sentence in the text that tells why bats are special.

COLLABORATE

Talk with a partner about how birds and bats are different. Find the part of the chart that tells about their wings. Draw a box around that part.

Bats like to make homes in caves and trees. These homes are called roosts. Lots of bats live together in a roost.

It is daytime. But the bats stay at home to sleep. They like to hang upside down.

Circle the two words that tell where bats make their homes. Write them here.

_____   _____

_____   _____

Underline the word that tells what bats' homes are called.

Write how bats like to hang.

_____

_____

COLLABORATE

Talk with a partner about what bats do during daytime.

Kay Maeritz/age fotostock

? **How does the way the author organizes information help you understand?**

Talk About It Reread the selection. Talk about how the chart helps you know more about bats and birds.

Text Evidence Write what you learned from the chart about how bats look.

Quick Tip

I can take notes about facts and information in the text as I read.

Body Part	What I learned about bats
Ears	
Covering	
Wings	
Legs	
Nose	

Write The author used a chart to help me know

_____

- -

? How does the hare's body help it?

COLLABORATE

Talk About It Talk about what you see in the painting and read in the caption. How is the hare's body like the bodies of the bats you read about?

Text Evidence Circle clues from the painting and text that show how the hare's body helps it.

Write The hare's body keeps it safe by

_____

- -

_____

- -

_____

Quick Tip

I can tell why the hare's fur changes colors using these sentence starters:

In the summer...
The fur changes to white to...

Read Together

image courtesy National Gallery of Art

The arctic hare's fur turns white in winter. This makes the hare hard to find in the snow.

Animal Teams

 How do the photographs help you understand how the animals work as a team?

Literature Anthology: pages 36–53

Talk About It Reread pages 42–43. Talk about what you see in the photographs.

Text Evidence Write what you learned from the text and photographs about the animal partners.

Tip of the Week

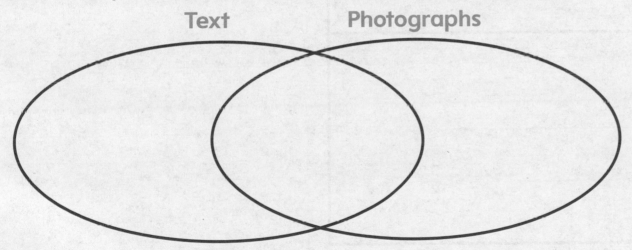

Text   Photographs

Write The photographs help me understand

_____

- -

_____

jessica lewis/Moment/Getty Images

Andrew

When I **reread**, I can look for clues in the text and the photos.

? **How does the author help you understand the information on these pages by asking questions?**

COLLABORATE

Talk About It Reread pages 44–47. Talk about the questions the author asks.

Text Evidence Use text clues to write answers to the questions that the author asks.

Question	Answer

Write The author asks and answers questions to

_____

- -

_____

Quick Tip

As I reread, I can use sentence starters to talk about the selection.

These pages tell about...

I learned that...

? **How does the author organize the information in this selection?**

COLLABORATE

Talk About It Reread pages 48–51. Talk about the information in the text on each page. Which animals are in the photos?

Text Evidence Write what you learned from the text and photos on each pair of pages.

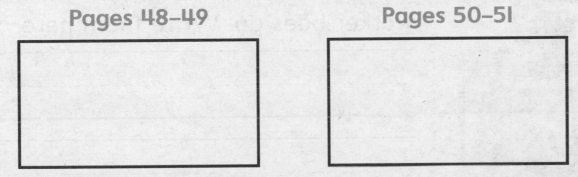

Pages 48–49

Pages 50–51

Write On each set of pages, the author uses facts and photographs to show

_____

- - - - - - - - - - - - - - - - - - - -

_____

Quick Tip

As I **reread**, I can find details about how animals help each other.

Your Turn

Which animal team is the most interesting? Why? Use these sentence starters:

The most interesting animal team is...

They are interesting because...

Go Digital!
Write your response online.

Busy As a Bee

Lots of worker bees help make honey. They help keep the hive clean, too.

Worker bees make wax cups called honeycombs.

Read Together

Reread and use the prompts to take notes in the text.

Draw a box around the words that tell what kind of bees this page tells about.

Circle the name of the wax cups that worker bees make.

Underline two things in the text that worker bees do. Write them here.

_____

- - - - - - - - - - - - - - - -

_____

_____

- - - - - - - - - - - - - - - -

_____

COLLABORATE

Talk with a partner about how many worker bees there are. Circle a word that helps you know.

Every hive has a queen bee.
She lays all the eggs.

A hive has drone bees, too.
A drone's job is to help the
queen make eggs.

A queen bee is with
her drones in the hive.

Photo by Jocelyn Winwood, NZ. Specialist: in nature shots/Getty Images

Underline the sentence that tells
what a queen bee does.

Circle the word that helps you know
drone bees work, too.

Write how drone bees help queen
bees.

_____

- - - - - - - - - - - - - - - - - - -

_____

COLLABORATE

Talk about the caption. Find the
queen bee and the drones in the
picture.

 How does the title "Busy As a Bee" help you understand the main idea?

COLLABORATE

Talk About It Reread the selection. Talk about the photos and the captions.

Text Evidence Write the jobs for each kind of bee in the chart.

Quick Tip

I can use the title to help me understand what the selection is mainly about.

Worker Bees	Queen Bee	Drone Bees

Write The title helps me understand that

_____

- -

_____

? How are these birds working together as a team?

Talk About It Talk about what is happening in the picture. How are these birds working together like the animal teams you read about?

Text Evidence Underline clues that help you figure out why these birds are a team.

Write The birds are a team because

_____

- - - - - - - - - - - - - - - - - - - -

_____

_____

- - - - - - - - - - - - - - - - - - - -

_____

Quick Tip

I can explain why flocks are a team using these sentence starters:

Birds flock together to...

The birds help one another...

It is safe to be in a big group. These birds flock together to stay safe.

Vulture View

 How do the text and illustrations help you know what vultures eat?

Monkey Business Images Ltd./Monkey Business/Getty Images Plus/Getty Images

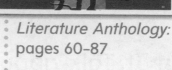

Literature Anthology: pages 60–87

 **Tip of the Week**

Talk About It How are the animals on pages 68-71 alike? How is the deer on page 75 different?

Text Evidence Write the names of the animals the vulture will not eat.

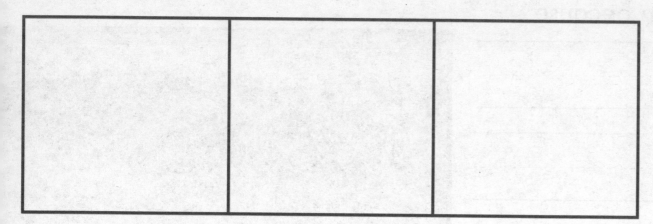

Write I learned that vultures eat

_____

- -

_____

David

When I **reread**, I find clues in text and illustrations.

? **How does the author use illustrations to teach you more about vultures?**

COLLABORATE

Talk About It Reread pages 76–79. Look at the illustrations and talk about what you see.

Text Evidence Tell what you learned about what vultures do when they eat.

CLOSE READING **Quick Tip**

As you reread, ask:

I can use these sentence starters to talk about vultures.

When vultures eat they…

After they eat they…

Words   Both   Illustrations

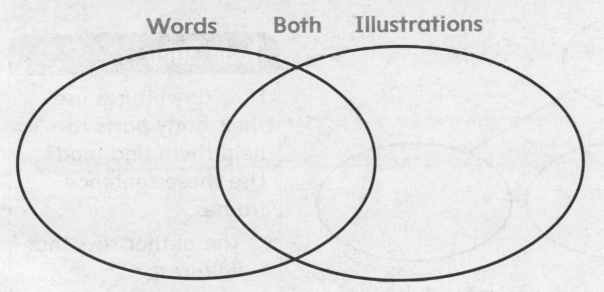

Write The illustrations show me that

_____

- -

_____

? **Why does the author repeat the word *down*?**

Talk About It Reread pages 82–83. Talk about what the author wants us to learn about vultures.

Text Evidence Name three things that go down at the end of the day.

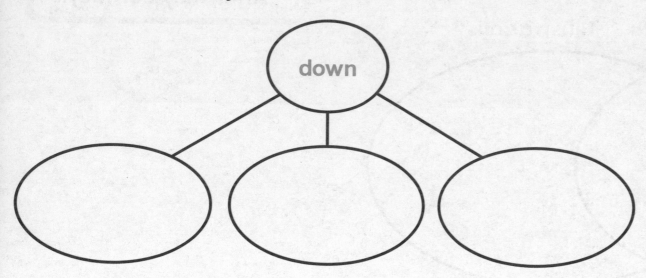

down

Write The author uses the word *down* to show

_____

- - - - - - - - - - - - - - - - - -

_____

Read Together

Quick Tip
CLOSE READING

The author chooses words to help me understand about vultures.

Your Turn

How do vultures use their body parts to help them find food? Use these sentence frames:

The author says that vultures...

This helps them find food because...

Go Digital!
Write your response online.

When It's Snowing

 How does the illustration help you understand the setting of the poem?

Talk About It Reread pages 90–91. Look at the illustration and talk about what you see.

Text Evidence Write clues from the illustration that help you know what it's like outside and inside.

Outside

Inside

Write The illustration helps me know

_____

- -

_____

Quick Tip

I can find clues in the text and illustrations that help me understand the setting.

? How do the sensory words help you know how the mouse survives in the cold?

Talk About It Reread pages 90–91. Talk about what is happening outside and inside the mouse's house.

Text Evidence Write the sensory words that help describe what is happening outside and inside.

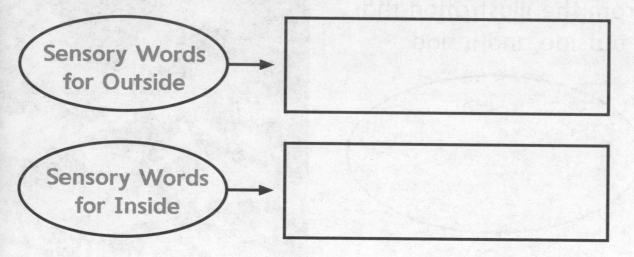

Sensory Words for Outside →

Sensory Words for Inside →

Write The poet uses sensory words to help me know the mouse

_____

- -

_____

Read Together

Quick Tip

I can use these sentence starters to talk about how the mouse survives.

The weather outside is…

Mouse's home is…

Mouse has…

How does the poet feel about the mouse?

COLLABORATE

Talk About It Reread the selection. Talk about the question the poet asks the mouse.

Text Evidence Write clues from the poem that show how the poet feels about the mouse.

What she calls it	What she asks it	How she describes it

Write I can tell that the poet

_____

- -

_____

Quick Tip

I can look at the author's word choices to understand how the author feels.

? **How is what vultures, mice, and orcas eat different?**

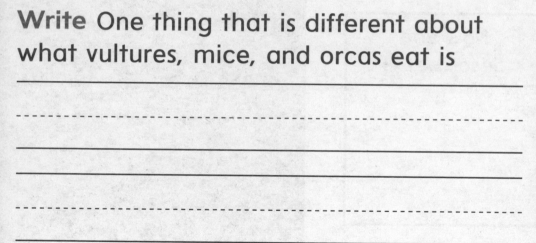

COLLABORATE

Talk About It Talk about what vultures, mice, and orcas eat. How do they all get food?

Text Evidence Circle clues that help you figure out what orcas eat.

Write One thing that is different about what vultures, mice, and orcas eat is

_____

_____

_____

_____

Read Together

CLOSE READING

Quick Tip

I can compare using these sentence starters:

Vultures eat...

Mice eat...

Orcas eat...

Tory Kallman/Moment/Getty Images

Orcas eat live fish and animals. They hunt for food in the sea.

Hi! Fly Guy

Literature Anthology: pages 92–123

? How do the text and illustrations help you know how Dad's feelings about the fly change?

Talk About It Reread pages 106–107. Talk about what Dad is doing on each page.

Text Evidence Use details from the illustrations and text to write what happens when Dad sees the fly.

 **Tip** of the **Week**

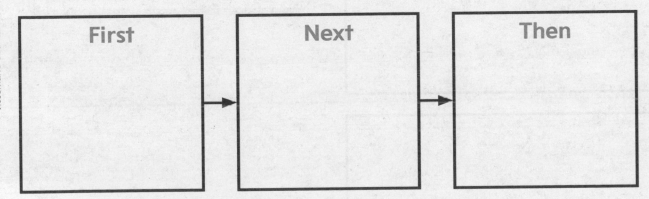

First	Next	Then

Write Dad's feelings change from thinking that

_____

- - - - - - - - - - - - - - - - - - -

_____

Amy

When I reread, I use clues from the illustrations to understand the characters.

Rosemarie Gearhart/Vetta/Getty Images

? **How do the illustrations help you know the judges' point of view?**

COLLABORATE

Talk About It Reread pages 112–115. Talk about how the judges look on page 112. What do they think about the fly?

Text Evidence Write details from the illustrations that help you know how the judges feel.

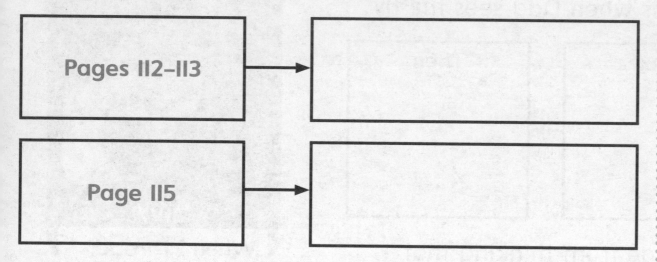

| Pages 112–113 | → | |
| Page 115 | → | |

Write The illustrations show that the judges

_____

- -

_____

Quick Tip
CLOSE READING

As I reread, I can use these sentence starters to talk about the judges.

At first the judges look …

The fly …

Then the judges look …

? **How does the illustration show that the judges have changed their minds about Fly Guy?**

COLLABORATE

Talk About It Reread pages 118–121. Talk about how the judges look on page 118.

Text Evidence Write the clues from the illustration that tell how the judges feel on page 121.

Quick Tip

I can look for clues in the illustrations about how characters feel.

Your Turn

Why do Buzz's parents and the judges change their minds about Fly Guy? Use these sentence starters:

At the beginning, they think...

Then Fly Guy...

At the end, they think...

Go Digital!
Write your response online.

Write The illustration shows that now the judges

_____

- -

_____

Unit 4 • Week 4 • Insects!   **123**

Meet the Insects

The Body of an Insect

All insects have six legs and three **body** parts. Insects have no bones.

The outside of an insect's body is hard. It **protects** the insect's body.

Most insects have antennas and wings.

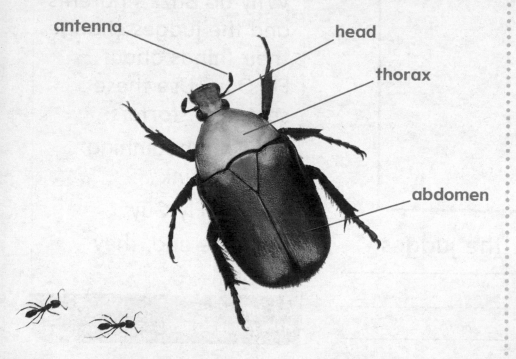

antenna

head

thorax

abdomen

Reread and use the prompts to take notes in the text.

Draw a box around the words that tell what the information is about.

Underline clues that tell what body parts all insects have.

Circle the sentence that tells you what most insects have.

Find the three main body parts that all insects have. Write the words.

_____ _____

- - - - - - - - - - - - - - - - - -

_____ _____

- - - - - - - - - - - - - - - - - -

_____

COLLABORATE

Talk about how the labels help you understand the insect body parts.

Insect Senses

Insects use their **senses** to find food. A fly smells with its antennas. It tastes with its feet. That's why flies like to land on food.

Insects do not see the same as we do. Many insects have more than two eyes. A grasshopper has five!

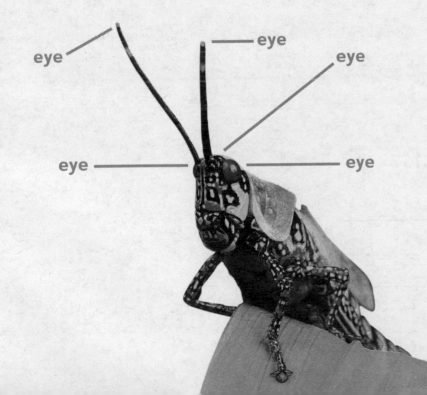

eye

eye

eye

eye

eye

Draw a box around the clue that tells you what the information is mostly about.

Find the word that tells what a fly does with its feet. Write it here.

_____

- -

_____

Write how many eyes a grasshopper has here.

_____

- -

_____

COLLABORATE

Talk with a partner about other things you can tell about this grasshopper from the photograph.

? Why does the author include photos of many different insects?

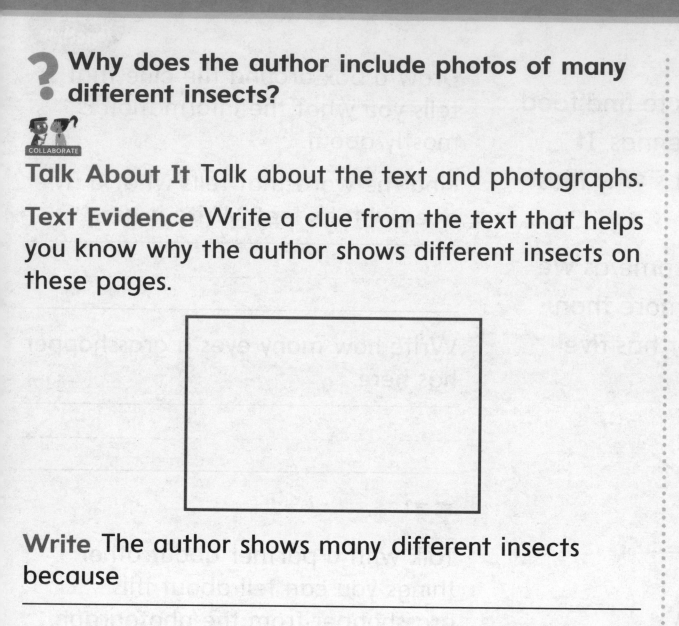

COLLABORATE

Talk About It Talk about the text and photographs.

Text Evidence Write a clue from the text that helps you know why the author shows different insects on these pages.

Quick Tip

I can use the photos to help me understand ideas in the text.

Write The author shows many different insects because

_____

- -

_____

? How do you know that a dragonfly is an insect?

COLLABORATE

Talk About It Talk about what the dragonfly looks like. How are its body parts alike and different from Fly Guy and the other insects you read about?

Text Evidence Underline clues that tell you what the dragonfly's body parts are. Circle them in the photograph.

Write One thing that is the same for all insects is that

_____

- -

_____

- -

_____

ChatchawalPhumkaew/iStock/Getty Images Plus/Getty Images

Quick Tip
CLOSE READING

I can describe dragonflies using these sentence starters:

Dragonflies have...
Dragonflies are insects because...

Read Together

A dragonfly's three body parts are easy to see in this picture. This dragonfly has a blue head and abdomen. Its thorax is green with black stripes.

Koko and Penny

? How do photo captions help you understand more about what you read in the text?

Literature Anthology: pages 130–137

Talk About It Reread pages 132–133. Talk about what Penny taught Koko to do.

Text Evidence Use clues from the captions to write what Koko's sign means in each of the photographs.

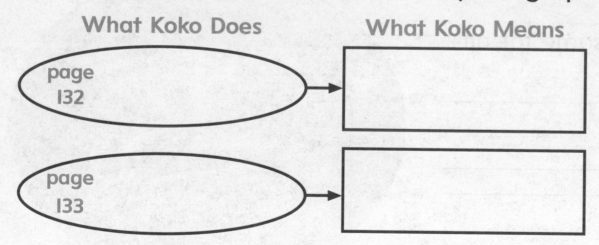

What Koko Does

page 132

page 133

What Koko Means

Write The photo captions help me understand.

 **Tip of the Week**

Hassan

When I **reread**, the photos and captions help me understand the text.

? **How does the way the author organizes ideas help you understand how Koko learned to use sign language?**

Talk About It Reread pages 132–133. Talk about how Koko learned words. What type of words did she learn first?

Text Evidence Use clues from the text to write words Koko learned first and later.

Koko first learned words like:

Koko later learned words like:

Write The author tells what happened

_____

- -

_____

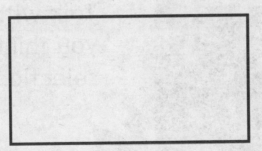

Your Turn

What benefits does Koko gain by learning sign language? Use these sentence starters:

Koko can ask for...

Koko can tell...

Signing helps Koko...

Go Digital!
Write your response online.

Saving Mountain Gorillas

Helen Gichohi lives in Kenya. She has a team that keeps gorillas like Koko safe.

Gorillas make a new bed of plants each night.

Reread and use the prompts to take notes in the text.

Where do gorillas sleep at night? Circle the clue in the caption.

Where do mountain gorillas probably live? Draw a box around the place name.

What does Dr. Helen Gichohi's team do? Underline the words.

COLLABORATE

Talk with a partner about what you think is the main idea of this selection.

? **Why do you think the author used photographs and captions in this text?**

COLLABORATE

Talk About It Talk about the information you can find in the photograph.

Text Evidence What do the captions tell you that the photographs and text do not?

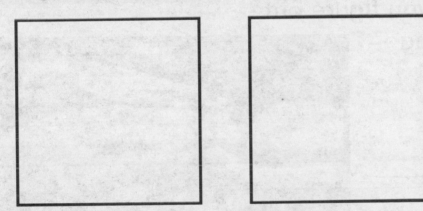

Write The author uses photos and captions to

_____

_____

_____

? **How did people and pigeons work together long ago?**

COLLABORATE

Talk About It A pigeon is a kind of bird. Talk about what birds can do that people cannot do. What have you read about people and animals working together to communicate?

Text Evidence Circle clues that help you figure out how the person in this photo is working with the pigeon.

Write Long ago, people worked with pigeons to

_____

- -

_____

- -

_____

Quick Tip

I can describe how people and pigeons worked together using these sentence starters:

A person attached...
The pigeon would...

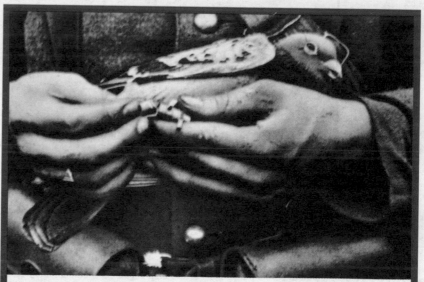

Long ago, pigeons carried important messages that were tied to their legs. They would fly and take the messages to people far away.

World History Archive/Alamy

132 Unit 4 • Week 5 • Working with Animals

A Lost Button

Literature Anthology: pages 140–153

? How does the author use dialogue to show that Frog is a good friend to Toad?

COLLABORATE

Talk About It Reread page 144. Talk about what is happening in the story.

Text Evidence Write three things Frog says that show he is a good friend.

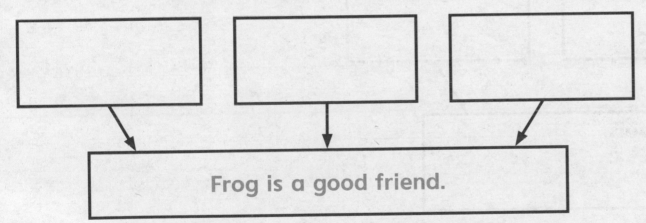

Frog is a good friend.

Write I know Frog is being a good friend when

_____

- -

_____

James

When I reread, I find clues to learn about the characters.

Ken Cavanagh/McGraw-Hill Education

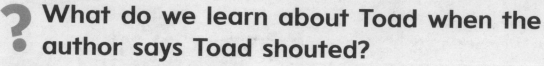

? **What do we learn about Toad when the author says Toad shouted?**

COLLABORATE

Talk About It Reread pages 148–149. Talk about what happens before Toad shouts.

Text Evidence Write three clues from the text and illustration that help you know how Toad feels.

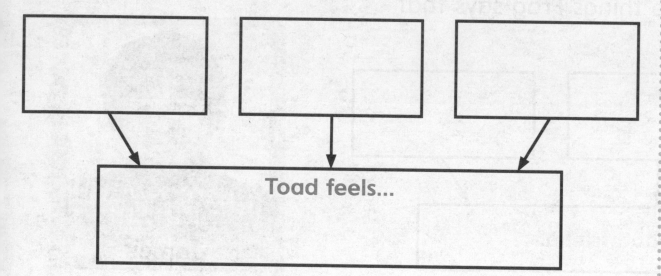

Toad feels...

Write Toad shouts because

_____

_____

Quick Tip
CLOSE READING

When I reread, I can use these sentence starters to talk about how Toad feels.

Toad feels...

After Toad finds the button...

? **How does the illustration help you understand how Toad is a good friend?**

COLLABORATE

Talk About It Reread page 151. Talk about what Toad says.

Text Evidence Write clues from the text and illustration that tell you how Toad feels about Frog.

Text	Illustration

Toad feels...

Write The illustration helps me know

_____

- -

_____

Quick Tip
When I reread, I can learn how characters feel by what they say.

Your Turn

In *A Lost Button*, do you think that Frog or Toad was the better friend? Why?

Use these sentence starters:

I think...

He was a better friend because...

Go Digital!
Write your response online.

Sort It Out

Some things are alike. Some are different. We can sort things by looking at what is the same about them. We can sort them by their size, shape, and color.

Find the buttons in this picture. Let's sort them!

Reread and use the prompts to take notes in the text.

Circle the word in the title that tells what the selection is about.

Underline the sentence that tells how to sort things.

Write three ways things can be sorted.

_____ _____

_____ _____

_____

COLLABORATE

Talk with a partner about different ways to sort the buttons. Circle the square buttons.

How many round buttons can you see?

How many square buttons can you see?

What other shapes do you see?

Add up the number of red buttons.

Are there more red or yellow buttons?

Can you find buttons with four holes?

How else could you sort these buttons?

Answer the first question here.

Answer the second question here.

Read the third question. Circle a button that answers the question.

COLLABORATE

Talk with a partner about other ways you can sort things.

Why do you think the author asks questions in "Sort It Out"?

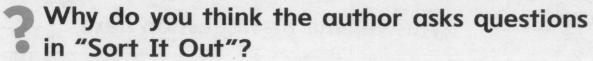

COLLABORATE

Talk About It Talk about how the questions help you understand the information.

Text Evidence Use the illustrations to answer the last three questions the author asks.

Read Together

Quick Tip
When I reread, I use clues to understand the author's purpose.

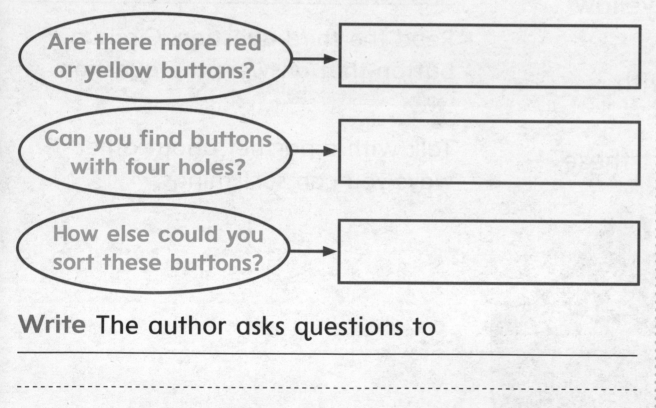

Are there more red or yellow buttons? →

Can you find buttons with four holes? →

How else could you sort these buttons? →

Write The author asks questions to

_____

_____

_____

? **How can you sort the animals in this poem?**

COLLABORATE

Talk About It Discuss what you learned about sorting in *A Lost Button* and "Sort It Out." What is the same about the lion and the bear in the poem?

Text Evidence Circle clues that show the lion and the bear are alike. Underline clues that show how they are different.

Write I can sort the lion and the bear by

_____

- -

_____

- -

CLOSE READING **Quick Tip**

I can classify using the sentence starters:

Only the lion...

Only the bear...

Both...

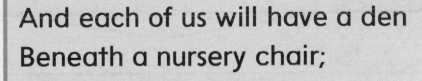

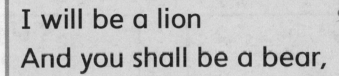
from **Wild Beasts**

I will be a lion

And you shall be a bear,

And each of us will have a den

Beneath a nursery chair;

And you must growl and growl

and growl,

And I will roar and roar.

— by Evaleen Stein

Kitten's First Full Moon

Literature Anthology: pages 162–193

? What clues help you know why Kitten thought the moon was a bowl of milk?

Talk About It Reread pages 164–165. Talk about what the first sentence means.

Text Evidence Write clues from the text that help you know why Kitten thinks the moon is milk.

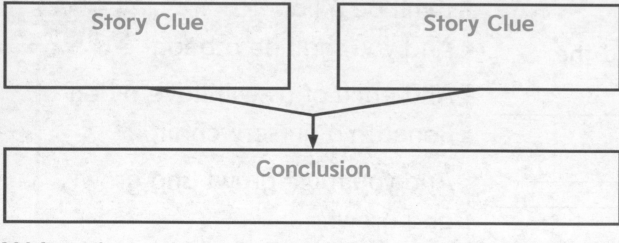

Story Clue	Story Clue

Conclusion

Write Kitten thinks it is a bowl of milk because

_____

- -

Read Together

CLOSE READING Tip of the Week

Carla

When I **reread**, I use clues in the illustrations to understand more about the story.

? Why does the author repeat the words "little bowl of milk"?

COLLABORATE

Talk About It Reread pages 170–173. Talk about what you see in the illustration. Whose point of view is the story told from?

Text Evidence Use clues from the text and illustration to write what Kitten does and thinks.

What Kitten Does	What Kitten Thinks

Write The author repeats "little bowl of milk" because

_____

- - - - - - - - - - - - - - - - - - - -

_____

As I reread, I can use these sentence starters to talk about what Kitten thinks and does.

Kitten wants to...

To reach it, she...

 How does the illustration help you understand what is happening in the story?

Talk About It Reread pages 180–181. Talk about what Kitten sees. What do you predict Kitten will do?

Text Evidence Write clues from the text and illustration that show what Kitten thinks.

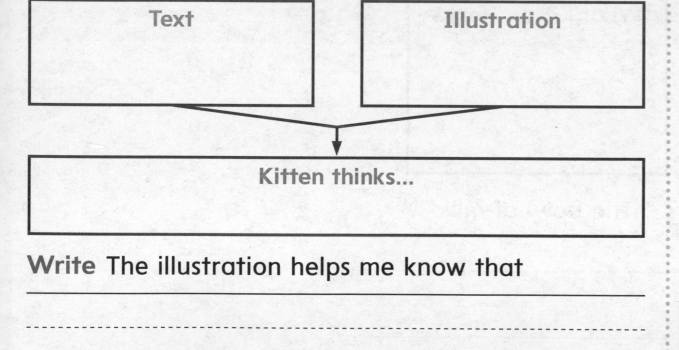

Text	Illustration

Kitten thinks...

Write The illustration helps me know that

_____

- -

_____

 **Quick Tip**

I find clues in the illustrations to help me understand the text.

Your Turn

Why couldn't Kitten drink the milk in the sky? How do you know? Use these sentence starters:

Kitten couldn't drink the milk because...

Kitten thought...

Go Digital!
Write your response online.

The Moon

People once thought the moon was made of cheese. They saw the face of a man in the moon.

Then telescopes helped us see the moon better. The telescopes showed hills and flat places. They showed craters, or big holes, too.

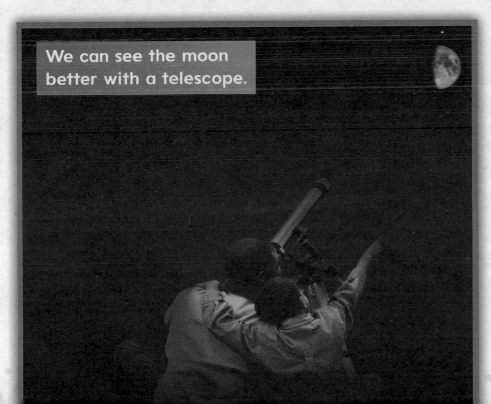

We can see the moon better with a telescope.

Reread and use the prompts to take notes in the text.

Underline two things that people used to think about the moon.

What helped people see the moon better? Circle the word. Put a star next to it in the photograph.

Write three things people could see on the moon with telescopes.

_____   _____

- - - - - - - - - - - - - -   - - - - - - - - - - - - - - -

_____   _____

- - - - - - - - - - - - - - -

_____

COLLABORATE

Talk with a partner about how telescopes helped us learn more about the moon.

Steve Cole/Photographer's Choice/Getty Images; (inset) somchaisom/iStock/360/Getty Images

Read Together

Then, in 1961, astronauts went to the moon. In 1969, other astronauts walked on it! They got a real close-up look.

Nothing grows on the moon. It is very rocky. Astronauts brought back moon rocks for us to see.

Maybe one day you will go to the moon, too!

Astronauts went into space and landed on the moon.

Underline the words that tell what happened in 1961.

Write two details about what the moon is like.

_____

_____

_____

_____

What did the astronauts bring back? Write it here.

_____

_____

COLLABORATE

Talk with a partner about how we know what the moon is like.

? **Why do you think the author tells what people thought about the moon?**

COLLABORATE

Talk About It Talk about what people thought the moon was made of.

Text Evidence Use your notes to write what people thought about the moon. Then write what they learned.

What People Thought About the Moon	Facts People Learned About the Moon

Write The author tells what people thought about the moon to show

_____

- -

_____

Read Together

? How is the sky different in the day than it is at night?

COLLABORATE

Talk About It Talk about how the night sky looked in the selections you read. Then talk about how the sky looks in this photo.

Text Evidence Label three clues in the photo that show how the daytime sky can be different from the nighttime sky.

Write The daytime sky is different from the night sky because

_____

- - - - - - - - - - - - - - - - - - - -

_____

- - - - - - - - - - - - - - - - - - - -

_____

Quick Tip

I can describe the daytime sky using these sentence starters:

The daytime sky is...

You can see...

This person paraglides in the open sky above the mountains.

Thomas Edison, Inventor

Literature Anthology: pages 202–219

 Why does the author include stories about Thomas Edison when he was young?

Talk About It Reread pages 206–207. Talk about Tom's worm experiment. Why did he think the girl would fly?

Text Evidence Use clues from the text to write what Tom was like as a boy and, later, as a man.

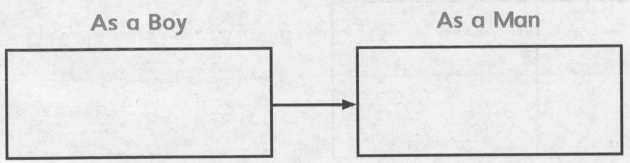

As a Boy	As a Man

Write The author has stories about young Thomas Edison to show

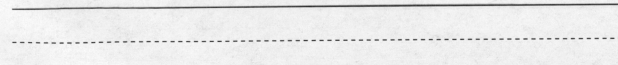

Emily

When I reread, I pay attention to stories about people to know more about them.

Diana Haronis dianasphotoart.com/Moment Open/Getty Images

? How do the text and illustrations help you know that Thomas Edison was a hard worker?

Talk About It Reread pages 211–213. Talk about what Tom is doing in the illustrations on these pages.

Text Evidence Use clues from each page. Write four things Thomas Edison did when he was young.

page 211	page 212	page 213

Write I know Thomas Edison was a hard worker because

_____

- -

_____

Quick Tip

As I reread, I can use these sentence starters to talk about young Tom Edison.

Tom liked to...

Tom made...

? **How does the author show that Tom kept trying new things?**

COLLABORATE

Talk About It Reread page 214. Talk about how people sent messages before there were telephones.

Text Evidence Write the steps Tom took that led him to invent new ways to use the telegraph.

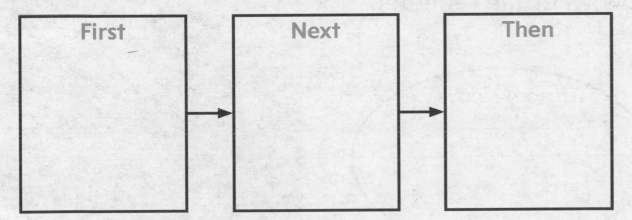

First

Next

Then

Write The author showed that Tom kept trying new things by telling about how

_____

- -

_____

Quick Tip

I can use clues from the text and illustrations to understand what I read.

Your Turn

Look at Chapters 1–2. What can you tell about what made Thomas Edison a good inventor? Include text evidence to support your answer. Use these sentence starters:

As a boy, Thomas Edison...

When he got older, he...

Go Digital!
Write your response online.

"Windshield Wipers"

? Why does the author repeat words in "Windshield Wipers"?

Talk About It Reread pages 222–223. Which words does the author repeat?

Text Evidence Write clues from the text and illustration that help you know what the repeated words mean.

The illustration shows...

The text says...

Write The author repeats the words to

_____

- -

"Scissors"

 Why does the author start and end the poem "Scissors" with a letter *X*?

COLLABORATE

Talk About It Reread pages 224–225 and look at the illustration. Talk about what scissors look like.

Text Evidence Write what the author says at the start and end of the poem to tell what X means.

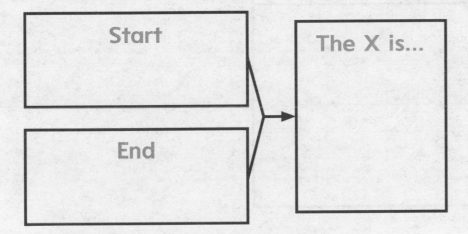

Start

End

The X is...

Write The author uses the letter *X* to

_____

- -

_____

CLOSE READING **Quick Tip**

I can use these sentence starters to talk about what scissors do.

Scissors look like...

When you open scissors...

? How does the author use sound words to help you understand windshield wipers and scissors?

COLLABORATE

Talk About It Reread the poems on pages 222–223. Talk about how windshield wipers and scissors move.

Text Evidence Write words from the poems that tell the sounds windshield wipers and scissors make.

CLOSE READING
Quick Tip
I can use sensory words to help me picture ideas in a poem.

Windshield Wipers	Scissors

Write The author includes sound words to

_____

- -

_____

? Why is the invention in the photo a good idea?

Talk About It Talk about the problems Thomas Edison solved with his inventions. How is the invention in the photo like the ones Thomas Edison came up with?

Text Evidence Circle two clues that help you know this is a good invention.

Write This invention is a good idea because

_____

- - - - - - - - - - - - - - - - - -

_____

_____

- - - - - - - - - - - - - - - - - -

_____

Quick Tip

I can explain about the invention using these sentence starters:

Some people need...
The invention helps...

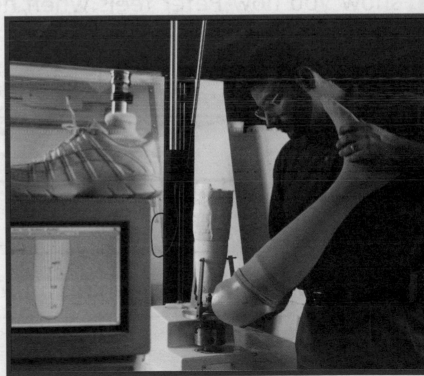

This artificial leg will help someone walk again.

Whistle for Willie

? How do the illustrations help you know how Peter feels after he whirls around?

Talk About It Reread pages 230–233. Talk about what Peter is doing.

Text Evidence Write text and illustration clues that show you how Peter feels when he stops.

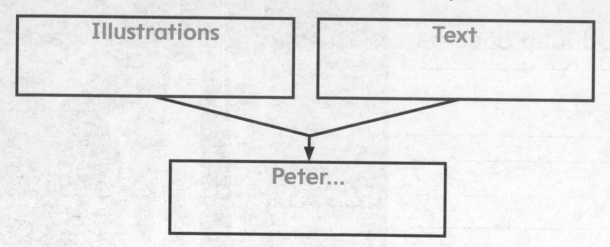

Illustrations	Text

Peter...

Write When he stops whirling around, Peter feels

_____

- -

_____

Literature Anthology:
pages 226–253

Tip of the Week

Jacob

When I **reread**, I can use the illustrations to understand what happens.

Ryan McVay/Photodisc/Getty Images

? **How does the author help you know that Peter won't give up trying to whistle?**

COLLABORATE

Talk About It Reread pages 234–237. Talk about what Peter's plan is. Why does he want to whistle?

Text Evidence Write what happens on these pages.

Quick Tip

As I reread, I can use sentence starters to discuss Peter's feelings.
When Peter...
I can see that...

pages 234–235

First	→	Next	→	Then

pages 236–237

First	→	Next	→	Then

Write I know that Peter won't give up because he

_____

- -

_____

? How does the author help you know how Peter feels when he finally whistles?

COLLABORATE

Talk About It Reread pages 246–248. Talk about what Peter does before he whistles.

Text Evidence Write what each clue tells you about how Peter feels.

Read Together

CLOSE READING

Quick Tip

I use clues from story events to know more about the characters.

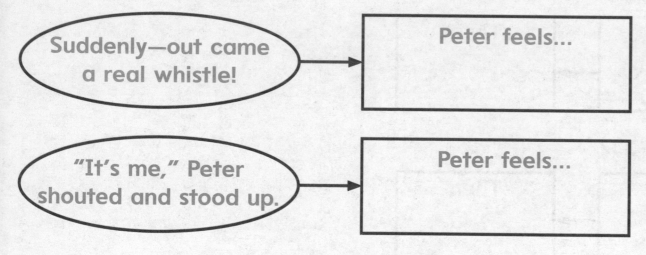

Suddenly—out came a real whistle! → Peter feels...

"It's me," Peter shouted and stood up. → Peter feels...

Write The author's words help me know that

_____

_____

Your Turn

Use what you know about Peter to write a new story about a time he learned to play a musical instrument or to sing a special song. Use these sentence starters:

Peter wanted to...

Peter tried...

Go Digital!
Write your response online.

Shake! Strike! Strum!

Shake, strike, strum! Instruments can be a lot of fun. Instruments make different kinds of sounds. Strike a drum. Rum-pum-pum. Strum a guitar. Plink, pling. Blow on a horn. Toot, toot. Shake it up! Some sounds are nice to hear. Others are not. But all sounds have two things in common: pitch and volume.

Rubberball/Chris Alvanas/Getty Images

Reread and use the prompts to take notes in the text.

Circle the words the author puts in the third sentence that tells what instruments do.

Underline names of instruments in the text.

What two things do all sounds have? Draw a box around the words. Write them here.

_____   _____

------------------------   ------------------------

_____   _____

COLLABORATE

Talk with a partner about the sound the boy in the photo is making. Circle the clue in the text.

Pitch is how high or low a sound is. When you whistle for a dog, you make a high-pitched sound.

Volume is how loud or soft a sound is. When you whisper in class, you make a low-volume sound.

Underline the sentence that tells what pitch is.

Write one kind of high-pitched sound here.

_____

- -

_____

Draw a box around the words that tells what volume is.

COLLABORATE

Talk with a partner about the photographs. Is the volume of the instruments high or low? Put a star next to the text clue that helps you know.

(l) Thomas Northcut/Photodisc/Getty Images; (r) RubberBall Productions/Getty Images.

? **Why is "Shake! Strike! Strum!" a good title for this selection?**

Talk About It Talk about how the children play the instruments in the photographs.

Text Evidence Write what you do to play each instrument and the sound it makes.

Instrument	How you play it	The sound it makes
Drum		
Guitar		

Write The author used the title "Shake! Strike! Strum!" because

_____

_____

Quick Tip
I can think about the words the author uses to understand the main idea.

? What makes the sounds at the end of the song? How do you know?

COLLABORATE

Talk About It Talk about the sound words. What are some sounds words you read in "Shake! Strike! Strum!"?

Text Evidence Underline clues that tell you what is making the sounds at the end of the song.

Write The sounds in the song come from

_____

_____

_____

_____

Quick Tip

I can explain the song using these sentence starters:

The car sounds like...
I think "crash beep beep" means...

Read Together

I Have a Car

I have a car, it's made of tin.
Nobody knows what shape it's in.
It has four wheels and a rumble seat.
Hear us chugging down the street.

Honk honk
Rattle rattle rattle
Crash beep beep.

Building Bridges

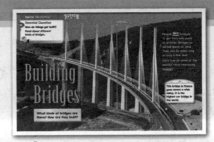

? How does the author use captions to help you understand the main idea?

COLLABORATE

Literature Anthology: pages 260–267

CLOSE READING
Tip of the **Week**

Talk About It Reread pages 260–263. Talk about what you see in the photographs.

Text Evidence Write what you read in each caption. Then write what kind of information the captions give.

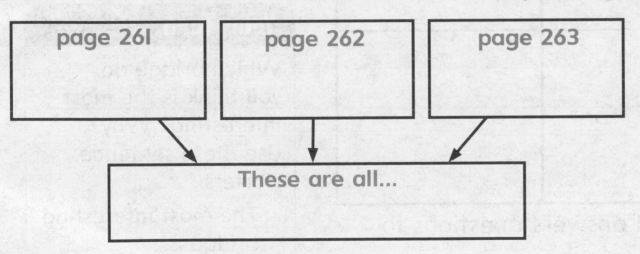

page 261	page 262	page 263

These are all...

Write The author uses captions

_____

- -

_____

Michael

I can use facts from captions to understand photographs and ideas in the text.

Ivanastar/iStock/Getty Images Plus/Getty Images

? Why does the author ask and answer questions in the text?

COLLABORATE

Talk About It Reread pages 264–266. Talk about the questions. Where can you find the answers?

Text Evidence Use clues from questions and answers to write what makes each bridge special.

Firth of Forth Bridge	Golden Gate Bridge	Rolling Bridge

Write The author asks and answers questions to help me

Read Together

Quick Tip

As I reread, I can use these sentence starters to talk about special bridges.

A truss bridge is...

Some bridges...

The Rolling Bridge...

Your Turn

Which bridge do you think is the most interesting? Why? Use these sentence starters:

The most interesting bridge is...

It is interesting because...

Go Digital!
Write your response online.

Small Joy

Tiny houses do not take a long time to build. Tiny houses do not cost a lot. And tiny houses do not take a lot of energy or materials. They are good for the earth!

Dee Williams

Tiny houses can go where their owners go!

Reread and use the prompts to take notes in the text.

Underline the words in the caption that tell where tiny houses can go.

Write three things that are good about tiny houses.

_____

_____

_____

_____

COLLABORATE

Talk with a partner about why tiny houses are good for the earth. Circle the clue.

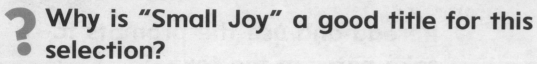

? **Why is "Small Joy" a good title for this selection?**

COLLABORATE

Talk About It Reread the selection. Talk about what *joy* means.

Text Evidence Write clues from the text and photos that tell what people like about tiny houses.

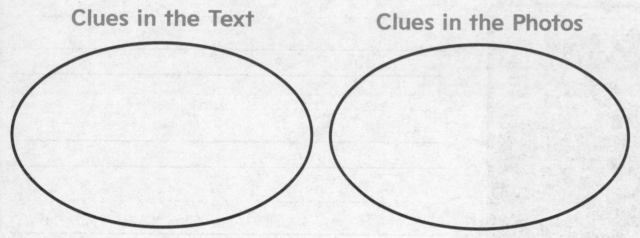

Clues in the Text

Clues in the Photos

Write "Small Joy" is a good title for the selection because

_____

- -

_____

? In what ways are big buildings and big bridges the same?

COLLABORATE

Talk About It Talk about how things get built. How is building a bridge like building the Capitol? Why is it important to build both?

Text Evidence Circle clues in the caption that help you know more about the U.S. Capitol building.

Write Making big buildings and big bridges

_____

- -

_____

_____

- -

_____

Library of Congress Prints and Photographs Division (LC-USZ6-1323)

Quick Tip

I can compare using the sentence starters:

Both bridges and buildings...

Buildings are different because...

It took a lot of years, money, and people to build the U.S. Capitol building. People do important work for our government there.

Click Clack Moo: Cows that Type

 Why does the author begin the cow's note with "Sorry"?

Literature Anthology: pages 270–293

COLLABORATE

Talk About It Reread pages 276–277. Talk about what Farmer Brown said.

Text Evidence Use clues from the text to write what Farmer Brown did and what the cows did.

 **Tip of the Week**

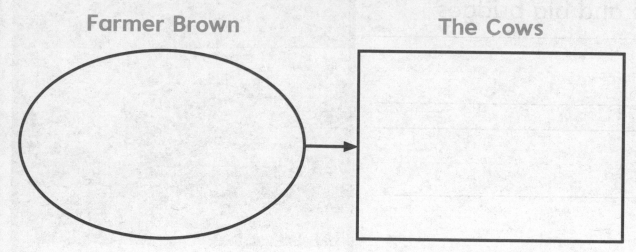

Farmer Brown   The Cows

Billy

Write The cows wrote "Sorry" because

_____

- -

I can use details from the story to understand what is happening.

? **How do the illustrations help you understand that the cows and hens are working together?**

COLLABORATE

Talk About It Reread pages 278–279. Talk about what happens in the illustrations.

Text Evidence Write clues from the illustrations that show what the cows and hens are doing.

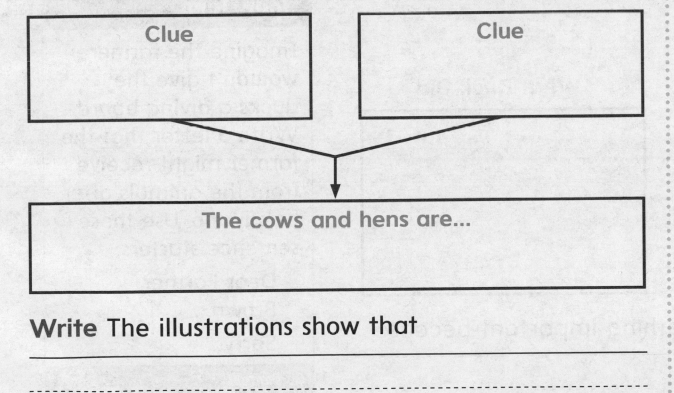

Clue	Clue

The cows and hens are...

Write The illustrations show that

_____

- -

_____

CLOSE READING
Quick Tip

As I reread, I can use these sentence starters to talk about how the cows and hens are working together.

The cows and the hens want...

They are working together by...

? How does the author let you know that Duck learned something important?

COLLABORATE

Talk About It Reread pages 291–293. Talk about what Farmer Brown wanted Duck to do.

Text Evidence Use clues from the text to write what Farmer Brown wanted and what Duck actually did.

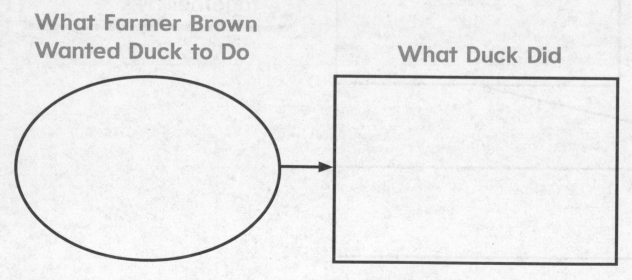

What Farmer Brown
Wanted Duck to Do

What Duck Did

Write Duck learned something important because

_____

- -

Quick Tip

I can use clues from the story to understand why characters do and say certain things.

Your Turn

Imagine the farmer wouldn't give the ducks a diving board. Write a letter that the farmer might receive from the animals after he says no. Use these sentence starters:

Dear Farmer Brown,...

Sorry...

Go Digital!
Write your response online.

March On!

How can people make their lives better? One way is to work together.

One hundred years ago, women in America were not allowed to vote. That meant they could not pick their leaders or help decide on laws and rules.

(bkgd) Superstock/Getty Images

Reread and use the prompts to take notes in the text.

Circle the sentence that tells how people can make their lives better.

Underline the words that tell the main problem in this selection.

When did this problem exist? Write the answer here:

_____

- -

_____

COLLABORATE

Talk with a partner about why this was a problem. Circle the clue.

I WISH MA COULD VOTE

Hulton Archive/Getty Images

Many women and men did not think this was fair. So they got together to protest. They marched and made speeches. They carried picket signs. People listened. In 1920, women got the right to vote.

Circle the word that tells what people got together to do.

How did people protest? Write the ways here.

_____

_____

_____

_____

_____

_____

_____

COLLABORATE

Talk with a partner about why the actions of the women and men helped to solve the problem.

? **How does the author organize information in this selection?**

Talk About It Talk about how a cause can have an effect. How does the author use cause and effect in this selection?

Text Evidence Use your notes and clues from the text to fill in the effects.

Quick Tip

When I reread, I think about how the author organizes information.

Cause	Effect
Women were not allowed to vote. →
Women and men protested. →

Write The author organizes the information by

_____

- -

? How are the children in the photo helping their community?

COLLABORATE

Talk About It Talk about how animals and people helped out in the selections you read this week. Then talk about what is happening in the photo.

Text Evidence Circle clues from the photo and caption that help you know how the children are helping their community.

Write The children are helping by

_____

- -

_____

_____

- -

_____

CLOSE READING

Quick Tip

I can describe how the children help by using these sentence starters:

   The children are...

   Parks need...

People can help by keeping parks clean.

Leland Bobbe/Digital Vision/Getty Images

Meet Rosina

Literature Anthology:
pages 302–321

? How do the photos help explain the way Hedy helps?

COLLABORATE

Talk About It Reread pages 310–311. Talk about how Hedy's job helps at school.

Text Evidence Write clues from the photos that show how Hedy is a good helper at school.

CLOSE READING

Tip of the **Week**

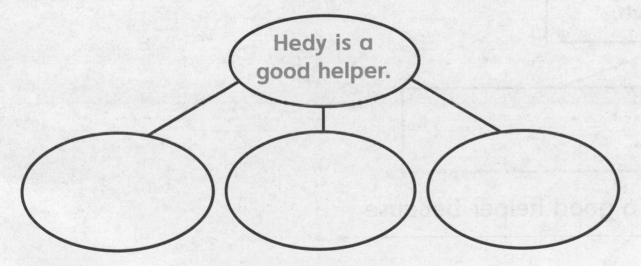

Hedy is a good helper.

Farah

When I **reread**, I use photographs to understand the author's words.

Write The photos show how

_____

_____

Laura Natividad/Moment Open/Getty Images

? How does the author help you know that Rosina's coach is a good helper?

COLLABORATE

Talk About It Reread page 315. Talk about what Rosina's team does.

Text Evidence Write clues from the text that help you know the team has a good coach.

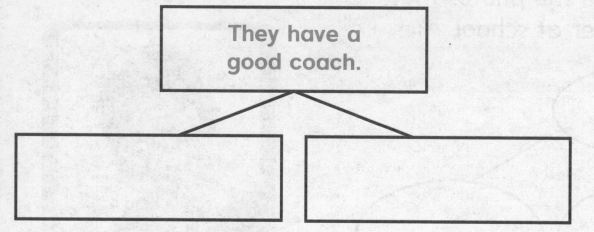

They have a good coach.

Write I know the coach is a good helper because

_____

_____

Read Together

Quick Tip

CLOSE READING

As I reread, I can use these sentence starters to talk about how the coach helps.

The team won a trophy, so...

All the players are...

? **What clues help you know Rosina's family helps one another?**

COLLABORATE

Talk About It Reread pages 316–317. Talk about what you see in the photographs.

Text Evidence Use clues from the photographs and text to write how each family member helps.

Mom	Rosina	Emilio	Dad

Write I know the family helps one another because

_____

CLOSE READING
Quick Tip
I can look for clues in the text and photographs.

Read Together

Your Turn

Rosina has a special community that works together. How do the people in your community work together to help you?

Use these sentence starters:

I get help from...

They help me by...

Go Digital!
Write your response online.

Abuelita's Lap

? **Why does the author use rhyming words in the poem?**

COLLABORATE

Talk About It Reread page 325. Talk about which lines rhyme.

Text Evidence Write the word pairs that rhyme in each part of the poem.

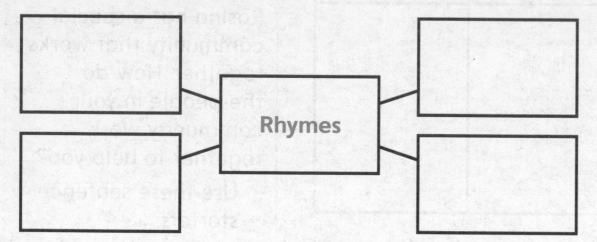

Rhymes

Write Rhyming words help make the poem

_____

- -

_____

Read Together

CLOSE READING
Quick Tip
When I reread, I notice the words that rhyme.

How does the title "Abuelita's Lap" help you understand the poem?

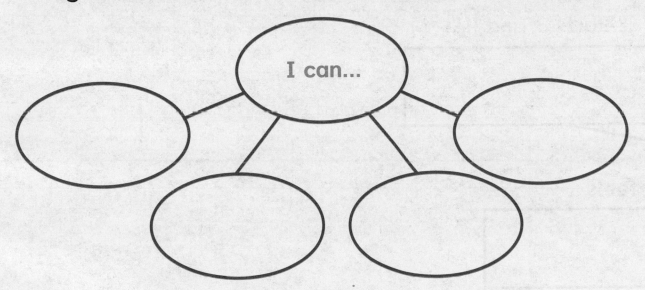

Talk About It Reread the poem. Talk about what the title means.

Text Evidence Write what the author talks about doing when he is in the place the poem is about.

I can...

Write The title helps me know

_____

- -

_____

Quick Tip

I can use these sentence starters to talk about the poem.

The poem tells about...

The author knows a place where...

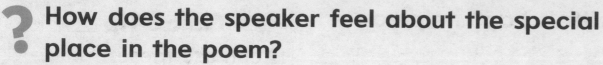
? **How does the speaker feel about the special place in the poem?**

COLLABORATE

Talk About It Reread the poem. Talk about the words the poet uses to tell how the speaker feels.

Text Evidence Write lines or words from the poem that tell how the speaker feels....

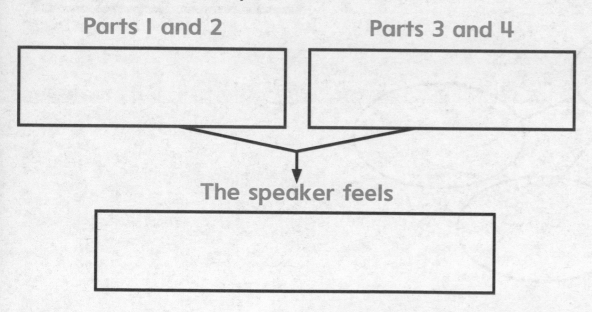

Parts 1 and 2

Parts 3 and 4

The speaker feels

Write The clues let me know that the speaker feels

_____

- -

_____

? How does the mother bird help her baby?

COLLABORATE

Talk About It How do family members help each other in *Meet Rosina* and "Abuelita's Lap"? What does the little birdie need help with?

Text Evidence Circle two clues that help you know how the mother bird helps.

Write Mother bird helps by

_____

_____

_____

Quick Tip

I tell about what the birdie says by using a sentence starter:

The little birdie tells the mother...

What Does Little Birdie Say?

What does little birdie say
In her nest at peep of day?
"Let me fly," says little birdie,
"Mother, let me fly away."
"Birdie, rest a little longer,
Till the little wings are stronger."
So she rests a little longer,
Then she flies away.

— Lord Alfred Tennyson

Rain School

? How do the text and illustrations help you understand what the first lesson is about?

Talk About It Reread pages 334–337. Talk about what you read and what you see in the illustrations.

Text Evidence Write clues from the text and illustrations that tell what the children are learning.

Text	Illustrations	The children learn...

Write The text and illustrations help me know that

_____

- -

_____

Literature Anthology: pages 326–355

BDLM/Cultura/Getty Images

 Read Together

 **Tip** of the **Week**

Hector

When I **reread**, I use the text and illustrations to know more about what happens.

? **How does the illustration show that the children are enjoying their work?**

Talk About It Reread pages 338–339. Talk about what the characters are doing in the illustration.

Text Evidence Write clues from the illustration that show how Thomas and his friends feel.

Clue	Clue

Thomas and his friends are...

Write I know the children enjoy the work because

_____

- -

_____

Quick Tip

As I reread, I can use these sentence starters to talk about how the children are enjoying their work.

Thomas is...

The other children are...

? How do the author's words help you know how the children feel about their school?

COLLABORATE

Talk About It Reread pages 340–341. Talk about what the school is like inside.

Text Evidence Write clues from the text that help show how the children feel about their school.

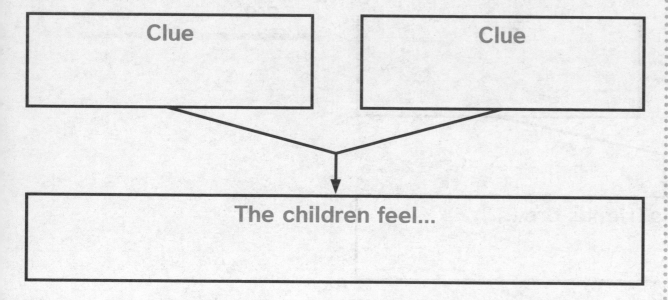

| Clue | Clue |

The children feel...

Write The words help me know the children are

_____

- -

_____

Quick Tip
CLOSE READING

I can use clues from the story to understand how characters feel.

Your Turn

What do the children in *Rain School* learn from their first lesson? Use these sentence starters:

Everyone worked...

The children learn...

Go Digital!
Write your response online.

Rainy Weather

Weather changes from day to day. Some days are sunny, and some days are rainy. When it rains, do you wish the rain would go away? You might, but we need rain.

Corbis/SuperStock

Reread and use the prompts to take notes in the text.

Underline the words that tell what weather does.

What kinds of days are there? Write the words here.

_____

- -

_____

_____

- -

_____

COLLABORATE

Talk with a partner about how you know the author will tell why rain is important. Circle the clues.

How Rain Helps

All living things need water. Rain helps plants grow, so that people and animals have food. Rain falls on ponds, lakes, and rivers. Then animals can drink water all year long. People need water to drink, too. We also use it for cooking and cleaning.

Circle the words that tell what this page is about.

Underline the sentence that tells why rain is important.

Write three things people do with water.

_____

_____

_____

_____

_____

_____

COLLABORATE

Talk with a partner about how rain helps animals. Circle the clues.

(r) Michael Krabs/imagebroker/age fotostock; (l) Blend Images/Alamy

? **How is the information in this selection organized?**

COLLABORATE

Talk About It Talk about how the headings help you know what each page is about.

Text Evidence Use clues from the text to write how the details tell more about the headings.

 Quick Tip

I can find clues to understand the most important details.

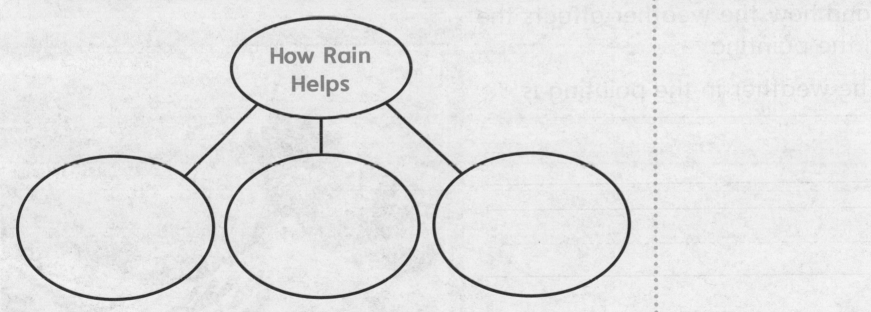

How Rain Helps

Write The author organizes the information by

_____

_____

? How are people affected by weather?

COLLABORATE

Talk About It Talk about what you see happening in the painting. How did the weather affect people in *Rain School* and "Rainy Weather"?

Text Evidence Circle three details that help you understand how the weather affects the boats in the painting.

Write The weather in the painting is

_____

_____

_____

Read Together

CLOSE READING

Quick Tip

I can describe what I see using these sentence starters:

The ocean is...

I see waves that...

This painting, *The Great Wave off Kanagawa* by Katsushika Hokusai, shows a huge wave next to boats.

Lissy's Friends

? How do the text and illustration help you know how Lissy feels?

Literature Anthology: pages 362–391

Talk About It Reread pages 376–377. Talk about what happens in the text and illustration.

Text Evidence Write clues from the text and illustration that help you know how Lissy feels.

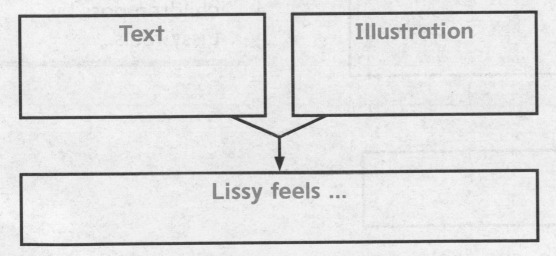

Text	Illustration

Lissy feels ...

Write The text and illustration tell me that

_____

Tip of the Week

Kate

I can use details from the text and illustrations to understand how a character feels.

Strickke/iStock/360/Getty Images

? How does the author show what happens as Lissy looks outside?

Talk About It Reread pages 378–379. Talk about what happens outside Lissy's window.

Text Evidence Write a clue from the text and from the illustration that shows what happens outside.

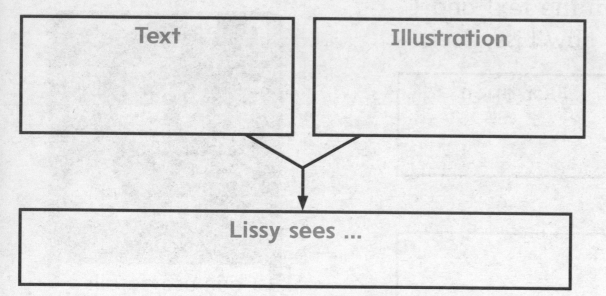

Text	Illustration

Lissy sees ...

Write When Lissy looks outside, she feels

_____

- -

_____

Quick Tip

As I reread, I can use these sentence starters to talk about what is happening outside and how it makes Lissy feel.

Lissy and the paper friends see...

When the other children pass by, Lissy feels...

? **What clues in the text and illustration help you know that things are different for Lissy now?**

COLLABORATE

Talk About It Reread pages 388–389. Talk about what is happening.

Text Evidence Write three clues from the text and illustrations that help you know things are different.

Clue	Clue	Clue

Write I know things are different because I see

_____

- -

_____

Quick Tip

CLOSE READING

I can use clues from the text and illustrations to understand what happens in the story.

Your Turn

Write a letter from Lissy to her paper friends telling them about how things are going now. Use these sentence starters:

Dear Paper Friends,...

Things are different now because...

Go Digital!
Write your response online.

Making Paper Shapes

See the crane made out of folded paper? Folding paper to make different shapes is called origami. People in Asia have made origami for hundreds of years.

Kids learn this art from their mothers, fathers, and grandparents.

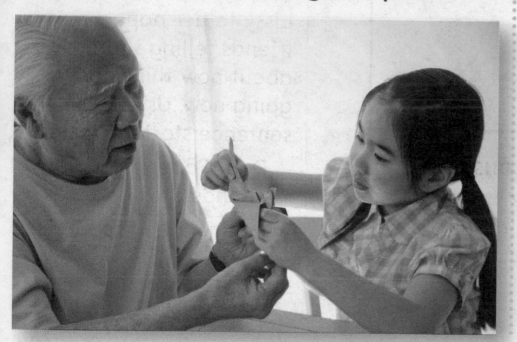

Reread and use the prompts to take notes in the text.

Circle the words that tell what the crane is made of.

Underline the sentence that tells what origami is.

COLLABORATE

Talk with a partner about reasons why origami is a tradition.

Blend Images/Ronnie Kaufman/Larry Hirshowitz/the Agency Collection/Getty Images

People in Japan make decorations for special days. One holiday is the Star Festival. Children sing songs and get treats to eat.

Families hang bright origami in the streets. Kids write wishes on slips of paper and hang them from sticks. They hope their wishes come true.

Write the name of the country this page is about.

_____

_____

Write the name of the festival.

_____

_____

COLLABORATE

Talk with a partner about what people do at the festival. Circle the clues.

? **How does the author organize the information in this selection?**

COLLABORATE

Talk About It Talk about the information on each page.

Text Evidence Write what the information on each page is about.

Quick Tip

I can find clues to understand how the author organizes information.

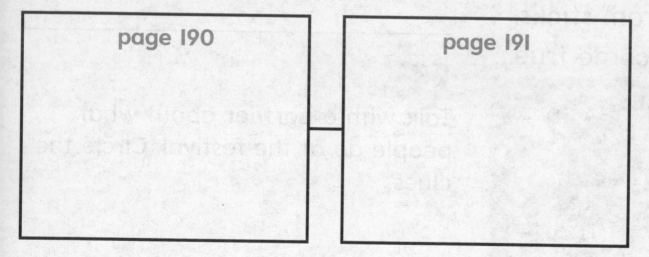

page 190

page 191

Write The author organizes the text to tell about

_____

- -

_____

? **How are the girls in the photo sharing a tradition?**

COLLABORATE

Talk About It Talk about the traditions people share in the selections you read this week. What tradition do the girls in the photo share?

Text Evidence Circle clues that help you figure out how the girls in the photo share a tradition.

Write I know the girls share a tradition because

_____

- -

_____

- -

_____

felix zaska Irish collection/Alamy

These girls perform Irish step dancing like their mothers and grandmothers did.

Happy Birthday, U.S.A.!

? How is the information organized on these pages?

COLLABORATE

Talk About It Reread pages 399–401. Talk about the question at the end of page 399.

Text Evidence Write what the information is about *before* the question. Write what the information is about *after* the question.

Literature Anthology: pages 398–405

Read Together

Before	After

Write The author organizes the information by

_____

- -

_____

 Tip **of the** Week

Grace

When I **reread**, I find clues in the text that tell when events took place.

Thomas Northcut/Photodisc/Getty Images

? Why does the author use dates in the text?

Talk About It Reread pages 402–403. Talk about how the author uses dates.

Text Evidence Use clues from the text to write what happened on the dates.

On July 4, 1776

On July 4 one year later

Write The author uses dates to show

_____

- -

_____

Read Together

Quick Tip

As I reread, I can use these sentence starters to talk about the events.

On July 4, 1776,...

One year later,...

Your Turn

What is the most important part of the Fourth of July? Why do you think so? Use these sentence frames:

On the Fourth of July, people...

The holiday is important because...

Go Digital!
Write your response online.

A Young Nation Grows

In 1776, our nation had just 13 colonies. About 2 million people lived here. Each colony later became a state. Look at the map of the colonies. Read the colony names below. Do you see any names you know?

Philadelphia

1776 Colonies

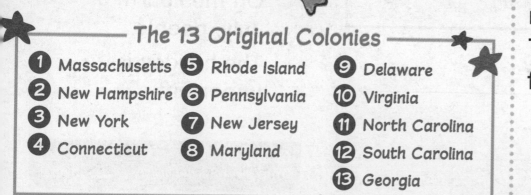

★ **The 13 Original Colonies** ★

1. Massachusetts
2. New Hampshire
3. New York
4. Connecticut
5. Rhode Island
6. Pennsylvania
7. New Jersey
8. Maryland
9. Delaware
10. Virginia
11. North Carolina
12. South Carolina
13. Georgia

Reread and use the prompts to take notes in the text.

Circle how many colonies there were in 1776.

Write how many people lived in the colonies.

_____

- - - - - - - - - - - - - - - - - - -

_____

Underline the sentence that tells what happened to the colonies.

COLLABORATE

Which colony is at the top of the map? Circle the answer on the map. Talk with a partner about how you found the answer.

? **How does the map key help you understand the map?**

Talk About It Look at the map of the colonies. Talk about the numbers that you see.

Text Evidence Compare what you can see on the map and the map key.

 Quick Tip

I can use map keys to find places on the map.

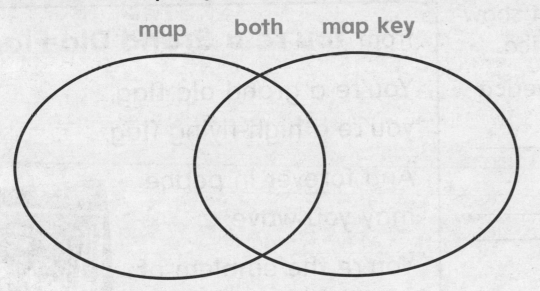

map   both   map key

Write I can use the map key to find

_____

- -

_____

COLLABORATE

? **How does this song celebrate America?**

Quick Tip

I can describe the song using these sentence starters:

The song is about...

It says America is...

Talk About It Talk about the ways people celebrate America in the selections you read this week. Then discuss what our flag stands for. Talk about what the words *grand* and *emblem* mean.

Text Evidence Circle clues that show how the song celebrates America.

Write The song celebrates America because

_____

_____

_____

_____

from **You're a Grand Old Flag**

You're a grand old flag,
you're a high-flying flag;

And forever in peace
may you wave;

You're the emblem of
that land I love;

The home of the free
and the brave.

— George M. Cohan